Praise for Steve Randazzo
and
Brand Experiences: Building Connections in a Digitally Cluttered World

"In today's increasingly cluttered brand environment, it takes a lot to grab people's attention. But Steve provides a step-by-step playbook for marketers to not only reach, but more importantly, connect with consumers. I only wish more of this real-world knowledge was taught in business schools to help aspiring CMOs understand how important consumer experiences are within the brand ecosystem."

Marc Abel
VP of Client Experience,
Weber Shandwick

"This is a must read for anyone looking to cut through the noise of today's marketplace and optimize customer engagement with their product or brand."

Greg Beach
VP Business Development
Event Strategy Group

"Explaining the relevance and importance of how experiential marketing can build a bridge to establishing long lasting emotional connections with customers and stakeholders is a difficult challenge. Brand Experiences does an excellent job of building that bridge through the life experiences of Steve in a relevant, meaningful and witty way."

Bruce Bowman
President, Play Products
KaBOOM!

"A great read for Marketers who are searching for a deeper level of connectivity with their most valued target consumers. In today's environment, going for the gag or the provocative (as is the trend) will fall short in static media environments. Here, Steve outlines a great thought process for eliciting visceral and deeply emotional connections with those we value through physical interactions."

Bob Fitzgerald
Senior Director, International Business Unit
Johnsonville, Inc.

"Brand Experiences is educational and actionable. It opens the doors to opportunities that have been hiding in your marketing blind spot. This book can double your company's marketing results in your key markets. The results will directly hit your bottom line. Take all the time necessary to digest its rich content and then implement your new brand strategy."

Stan Herman, MBA, ChBC
Business and Retirement Certified Coach

"If your current marketing strategy is loaded with worn out status quo elements, Brand Experiences will show you how to think differently and start seeing tangible results."

Jeremy Jepson

"Brand Experiences provides a quick and comprehensive understanding of Experiential Marketing's important and growing place in today's business environment. Put together in an easily accessible manner, it contains great stories that will help you remember the valuable information. I have known Steve for about 20 years, do yourself a favor - read this book."

Greg Johnston
President
Thumbs Up Marketing

"Steve's insights into how products and brands can connect on a one-to-one basis with end users and consumers is a great playbook for any company looking to do five-star outreach."

Bill Kahl
Executive Vice President of Marketing,
ShurTech Brands

"Brand Experiences truly illustrates today's marketing struggles. The key lies in tying every initiative to revenue, and continually testing effectiveness, measuring impact and fine-tuning programs. If there is no ROI planned, why would you do it?"

Melissa Lackey
President and CEO
Standing Partnership

"This book is a great read for anyone who wants to understand how to gain trial, awareness, and new sales for their brand."

Rod Mills
Regional Sales Manager
Invacare

"Deciding to build your brand through relevant, engaging and memorable experiences is the easy part. Knowing HOW can seem far more difficult. In Brand Experiences, Steve calls on over 30 years of experience to show you how to unlock this powerful brand building tool."

Paul Verdu
VP Sales and Marketing
Tenth and Blake Beer Company at MillerCoors

BRAND
EXPERIENCES
BUILDING CONNECTIONS IN A
DIGITALLY CLUTTERED WORLD

STEVE RANDAZZO

ISBN 978-1-7338745-0-2 (Hardback)

ISBN 978-1-7338745-1-9 (eBook)

PAIPHEN
publishing

BRAND
EXPERIENCES
BUILDING CONNECTIONS IN A
DIGITALLY CLUTTERED WORLD

Dedication

This book is dedicated to my immediate family first and foremost: Patti, Paige, Stephen, Louie (fur baby), mom, dad, Vicki and Gary.

Without all my focus on the kids and their activities, this book would have been written 10 years ago! It is not a coincidence that the book gets completed the first year they are both in college.

It is also dedicated to all the great office team and field staff I have been fortunate to attract to my company since 1995. I recognized very early that "work as a team, win as a team" would be core to our success.

And, finally, a big thank you to all the amazing clients who have trusted this independent experiential marketing agency out of St. Louis to be the face of their brand all across the United States and into Canada.

I'm a lucky guy.

CONTENTS

Foreword

Over the past 20 years, my job has been to help brands tell their stories in new and different ways. When brands want to transcend the expected and turn some heads, they call my shop.

Our job is to wow them, delivering a little dose of magic absent from the traditional marketing plan. After getting briefed by our clients, we fill whiteboards, notepads, trash cans, and napkins with gestating ideas. We eventually give presentations, deliver ideas, exchange high fives and handshakes, and sometimes even raise a few glasses in celebration.

Once we're far away from our clients and removed from the sweet victory of selling an exciting new program, reality sets in. We quietly ask ourselves, "How the heck are we going to pull this off?"

More often than not, the answer is "Call Steve."

We need a double-decker bus with a 4D immersive movie theater and a full karaoke studio for LG.
    "Call Steve."

We need a road-legal, larger-than-life, fully functional Tonka dump truck to promote Tonka's 60th Anniversary.
    "Call Steve."

We need to create a professional-grade mobile locker room for Gatorade befitting of sports royalty, and we need to bring it to high school powerhouses nationwide. And we need it in 40 days.
    "Call Steve."

While each of those examples is true, it's a tad belittling to suggest that Steve and his crew at Pro Motion simply helped us realize our ideas — they did far more. They helped mold our programs, pressure-testing them and suggesting improvements along the way. Steve was and is an invaluable extension of our team.

It's thrilling that Steve has taken the plunge to distill his secret sauce of marketing expertise and share it with the world. The simple reality, as you'll learn, is that consumer spending on live experiences and events has increased 70 percent over the past three decades. Just about everybody is sharing their experiences on social platforms — not just Millennials and members of Generation Z. Going further, weaving experiences into marketing has the proven potential to boost consumer satisfaction with a material purchase.

Marketers must find ways to leverage these dynamics. The following pages will illuminate the path forward for action-oriented brand managers, publishers, and agencies that want to move the needle. Better yet, they'll take this journey in Steve's trademark style: plain-spoken truths, a complete lack of BS, real-world knowledge, a spark of creativity, and a dash of inspiration.

Dive in and see how Steve's wisdom can elevate your marketing into an experience that's unforgettable and demands to be shared.

—Tres McCullough
Co-founder and Chief Engagement Officer
Fathom Communications

Finding My Roots in Experiential Marketing

"Tell stories. Always tell stories." —*Guy Kawasaki*

The term "experiential marketing" didn't begin to make the rounds in professional circles until about 15 years ago. When we started Pro Motion in 1995, we were in the event marketing business. The vocabulary and meaning changed somewhere along the way, bringing us to our current focus: how experiences can shape brands and emotionally connect them with their target audiences.

I've been working in marketing for more than 30 years. While "experiential" is a relatively recent term, the power of experience and storytelling is anything but new.

Despite experiential marketing's rising popularity, many individuals outside of the marketing world misunderstand it. Many of my connections are familiar with event marketing, but few of them have heard of experiential — even fewer understand the distinction between the two.

Some ask me if I'm responsible for PR stunts or viral gags. While I wouldn't describe it that way, they aren't far off with their thinking. These events certainly fall under the experiential marketing umbrella, but it's important to understand that experiential is anything *but* a gimmick: It's the seed of an emotional connection that can last a lifetime.

Experiential marketing's appeal is rooted in how visitors (potential customers) naturally feel involved with a brand's cultivated experience. This allure has a lot to do with how I stumbled into the industry. At first, I just wanted to be a part of something bigger — the baseball world.

I focused on marketing and public relations in college, and I was able to land a job with a Major League Baseball team after graduation. It took nearly three months to convince the general manager to let a 22-year-old join the front office, but I eventually won them over. I got my first taste of what would later become experiential marketing while serving as a marketing assistant with the Kansas City Royals.

During those formative years, everything that happened on the field (aside from actual baseball) was my responsibility — starting with ceremonial first pitches. Most people don't realize how much coordination is required to get someone to run out onto the field and throw a baseball. Despite this challenge, I was able to keep things on track game after game. I later oversaw individuals who performed the national anthem, which involved all sorts of new logistics. As the months passed, I handled larger and more complex events until I eventually was responsible for the overall atmosphere of the stadium.

It was an incredible amount of work. Looking back, it was the greatest job I would never want to work again. Those experiences taught me how to wear multiple hats and how to connect with a crowd through the magic of shared experiences. They also exposed me to different levels of fanaticism.

After an incredible time with the Royals, I left my job to move back home to St. Louis. I took a position with Vess Beverages, a regional company that spanned about 35 states. At the ripe old age of 23, I took over as the company's director of marketing. I grew it from a department of one (myself) to a 12-person staff four years later.

Vess Beverages hosted events throughout the Midwest, which enabled me to do a bit of everything. We used a Vess-branded parachute team to deliver the game ball for a University of Missouri football game, bought a 1942 fire truck and used it to participate in local parades, coordinated four Vess hot air balloons, and dispatched countless concession trailers stocked with Vess products and inflatables wherever we wanted to make an impression. The chaos and craziness that often accompanies experiential marketing soon became second nature.

When I left Vess Beverages, I wanted to build my résumé and found that opportunity with Ralston Purina, where I spent four years marketing everything from Wonder Bread to Chex Mix to Dog Chow. I was perfecting my traditional marketing skills, but I began to miss the excitement of experiential. To scratch that itch, I started consulting on the side for McCann-Erickson Event Marketing to craft a baseball-themed national promotion for Nabisco.

In what was probably one of the coolest campaigns I've built in my career, we put together a program called the Nabisco All-Star Legends. Our star-studded roster included five legends from the Baseball Hall of Fame and about 40 other former MLB players. I was young and childless, so I was able to travel the country and coordinate dozens of exhilarating events with MLB legends on behalf of Nabisco.

After about two years with McCann-Erickson, I was ready to start my own company. While I had never pursued it directly, my early years in the marketing world made me uniquely qualified to focus on experiential marketing. I was good at it, enjoyed it, and wanted to explore new horizons of experiences. Pro Motion was born in 1995, and has spent the past two decades leading emotionally connective experiential campaigns.

The Power of Experiential

I recently spoke with one of our clients about the emotional connections her brand has been able to achieve with customers as a result of our work together. She put it best: "You can't get those kinds of experiences and connections through digital or print."

She's right. The only way to create those strong, enduring connections is to reach out to customers and engage in face-to-face conversations.

This client isn't the first person to discover the power of experiential marketing. According to Event Marketer and Mosaic,[1] 86 percent of brands planned to execute more — or at least the same number — of events and experiential campaigns in 2018 than in 2017. Rest assured, that figure has grown in recent years. Experiential marketing forms a unique connection that is too easily lost in today's world of digital advancements. That real "A-ha" moment — or at least the opportunity for that moment — is extremely rare online, but it happens multiple times a day in our industry.

For example, my company works quite a bit with Tractor Supply Company. We coordinate experiential events at state fairs and rodeos, often bringing along a taxidermic bull and other fun activities. Visitors sit on the stuffed bull, laugh, and smile wide for a fun picture. To extend the experience, we allow attendees to share those photos electronically with friends and family — some people even use the images on their Christmas cards. No lie.

My family struggles to figure out what to put on our *own* holiday cards, but the power of experiential marketing enables me to help hundreds (or even thousands) of people create their holiday greetings. Those cards are highly personal, and each one features a unique experience that promotes the Tractor Supply Company brand.

This success is noteworthy, but it isn't an isolated event. Bizzabo found that 95 percent of marketers agree that live events create valuable personal connections in a society obsessed with the digital world.[2] Even as digital campaigns become more sophisticated, 76 percent of consumers say they will only advocate for brands that provide great personal experiences.[3] What better way to encourage that advocacy than through a personal experience that warrants consumer chatter?

Experiential marketing has the power to create authentic audience connections like no other modern media. While digital outreach is important, the best way to create brand advocates and secure a company's future is by creating a connective and deeply emotional experience.

The Perfect Match: Experiential Marketing and Emotional Connections

Now more than ever (especially as we move into a digital future), meaningful consumer connections are crucial to brand success. It's easy to send a text or a tweet, but those messages are rarely memorable.

Think of it this way: I don't remember anything I read on Twitter yesterday. By online standards, those tweets may as well have happened last year. However, I *do* remember playing golf with my friends last week. I remember hanging out together after we finished our round. I remember talking and laughing, and I remember what we talked and laughed about. Those were *experiences* that, even if I tried, I couldn't forget. Would you like to go to a concert and experience the sights, sounds, and smells of the event, or would you rather watch smartphone videos from a friend who attended?

Disclaimer: While experiential marketing campaigns can forge emotional connections, this result is no small feat. Before you throw together an experience and expect success to follow, you must first understand the personalities and behavioral tendencies of your target audience. Digging up that information can be a hit-or-miss process, but you are more likely to capture the attention (and hopefully the hearts) of your audience members through experiences than via direct mail or social media.

Humans are complex creatures. Fortunately, most of the personality traits that drive us fall in one of five buckets: openness, conscientiousness, extraversion, agreeableness, and neuroticism.[4] Conscientious people are easy to be around, and neurotic individuals obsess over details. Extroverts and agreeable people are both inherently social, but an openness-driven personality tends to vary widely from one consumer to the next. If it's not apparent, there is more science to this industry than some might think.

Your audience members likely share a few tendencies in these categories. If you appeal to them on their terms, they are more likely to listen to your message. If you miss the mark, though, they will see you as either a nobody or an adversary. As you design your experience, don't build what you think will work for a general population — craft the story that works best for the specific personality makeup of your brand's target audience. You might catch fewer eyes, but the ones that pay attention will be far more likely to convert.

This focus on personality works because humans are emotional creatures. Modern scientific research suggests that emotion motivates all consumers, even executives at B2B companies. We might like to think of ourselves as logical, but we are more likely to be attracted to brands that make us *feel* special or that share one of our personal goals.

By tapping into these emotional motivators, you can lay the foundation for purchase, loyalty, and brand fanaticism. That final stage of advocacy is essential to long-term profits, by the way. One-time customers are nice. Loyalists are dependable. Fanatics (and advocates), though, are 52 percent more valuable than customers who are "highly satisfied" with a brand.[5]

Consumers don't forge emotional connections on a lark, though. Digital marketers track and target their every online movement, and thousands of advertisements compete for their limited attention. As a result, audiences have become adept at ignoring anything that doesn't catch their interest in nanoseconds. To break through that noise and spark authentic passion, marketers must reach through the digital veil and give consumers a real-life experience — a story — to remember.

Educate, Engage, and Inspire for Experiential Marketing Success

At this point, I hope you're at least intrigued by the value of experiential marketing. Done correctly, it empowers brands to form lasting emotional connections with consumers. But before you can tap into this power, you'll need to know how to strategize, create, and execute experiential activations successfully.

The following nine chapters are here to help you do just that. After reflecting on my 30 plus years of experience in the marketing world, I wrote this book to explain not only how but *why* you should target your audiences through experiential marketing.

To better illustrate the process, I've broken the following chapters into three parts: educate, engage, and inspire. Whether it's a TV commercial, a print ad, or a social media post, every marketing initiative seeks to *educate* consumers on a topic, *engage* their interest, and *inspire* them to act — in fact, 85 percent of people are likely to buy following an event or experience.[1] These sections will help you move beyond your desire to connect with consumers and help you forge meaningful relationships through experiential marketing. Let's get started!

PART I

EDUCATE

CHAPTER 1

Make a Splash

"People do not buy goods and services. They buy relations, stories, and magic." —Seth Godin

Whether your brand has just created its first product or you have strong, existing offerings already on the market, you need to drive sales, elevate awareness, and educate consumers. Your marketing team might adore your product, but it's time to get consumers to fall in love with it.

Among many marketing options, you could run a commercial on television. After all, commercials have been the gold standard for advertising since the Super Bowl made advertising a spectator sport. When you ask people about their favorite commercials, everyone has something to say. Given this context, it's easy to imagine the impact a few strategically placed 30-second spots could have.

You could be like the big car companies, giving viewers a glimpse at the self-driving technology they crave. You could take a page from IBM's book and speak to business owners, throwing out buzzwords like "blockchain" and "artificial intelligence on the cloud" to demonstrate your technological know-how. You could even go the sappy route, showing a dad who wants to go home to his kids but is unable to do so without your incredible new product.

You could also live in the real world. Television advertising viewership is dwindling. With consumers dumping their cable providers in droves, it seems odd that Super Bowl commercial prices would be on the rise. TV's share of ad spending in the U.S. is on pace to dip under 30 percent by 2021[6], and that revenue isn't coming back (unless the internet suddenly disappears). Consumers who haven't cut the cable cord rely on DVRs to skip commercials, and 64 percent[7] of viewers stare at their smartphones while watching shows. In short, people just don't watch commercials anymore.

Even if your commercial does garner some attention, the dwindling number of individuals who keep their eyes glued to their screens during commercial breaks rarely fit anyone's target demographic. How many young adults actually pay attention to beer commercials that show young adults partying? And what are the odds that any of them will buy a beer because a commercial told them to? In the same vein, how many decision makers at major corporations do you think take their cues on IT infrastructure from commercials aired during "Monday Night Football"? Authentic connections in commercials are few and far between, even among people who pay attention.

I have spent decades watching television. But even after hours upon hours of commercials, I can recall only a few moments when an advertisement actually swayed my purchasing decision.

About 19 years ago, before the internet changed the world, my brother-in-law died in a car crash. My kids were young at the time, and this devastating experience convinced me that driving an unsafe car was not an option. I made it my mission to buy the safest car on the market.

When no one was willing to sell me an armored tank, I had to pick from the traditional options.

These concerns were bouncing around the back of my mind one day when I saw a Volvo ad on TV. The commercial showed a child sitting in a car seat in the back of the car, laughing in the sun, while his father drove. The father smiled comfortably with the knowledge that, no matter what happened, his Volvo had the safety features he needed to keep his family safe. The commercial asked: "If gold and silver travel in armored cars, how do we protect a child's dreams?"

That message resonated with me. I wanted the car with the best safety features on the market. I wanted to protect my family from further upheaval. My mind was fully open, and Volvo told me *what* I wanted to hear *when* I wanted to hear it.

Before I saw that commercial, I had no idea which car was the safest option (Google wasn't in my pocket at the time). But after that experience, I went right out and bought a dependable Volvo station wagon — and three more Volvos as the years went on. The brand earned my business by engaging with me at exactly the right time, creating an emotional connection at a moment in my life when I needed one.

All these years later, that Volvo commercial remains one of a few ads that drove me to make a purchase — one success across decades of wasted marketing dollars. And that was before smartphones and instant product reviews became part of daily life. Technology has made the already rare commercial success even more unlikely. We tune out new information from banner ads, television commercials, and other sales pitches. If I saw that commercial today, I might pull out my smartphone, review the safest cars, and pick a Toyota instead.

To convert new customers, businesses must reach target audiences when their minds are open — and nothing captures attention like an authentic, real-world experience.

Find Open Minds

Experiential marketing eliminates the question of whether your target audience is paying attention. When you're right in front of people and allowing them to interact with a new product, let the strength of your offering speak for itself.

Much like real estate, experiences are all about location, location, location. According to the Harvard Business Review[8], people tend to be more receptive to new information when they're in a familiar environment. Unfamiliar situations induce stress, forcing our brains to focus more on survival than absorbing new information.

Imagine this scene at your local playground: Several parents are engaged in the Saturday ritual of small talk while their children play nearby. In this familiar setting, the parents are comfortable and open to relevant experiences. During yet another discussion about the fine art of parenthood, a marketer appears with nutritious yogurt samples. This marketer is a representative of a company that promotes better food options for children, and he offers the parents a few samples to see whether their kids like the product. Thanks to the positive and familiar environment — where parents have open minds that are not bogged down by their to-do lists or concerns about their children's safety — along with the relevance of the experience, the parents have no problem accepting the offer. After all, they have nothing to lose and everything to gain.

This hypothetical situation works well because relevant experiences don't feel like advertisements or marketing initiatives. When someone offers snacks to parents of young children at a playground, the parents interpret that gesture as helpful and sincere. After the experience, the parents will likely remember the snack brand in a positive light (even if their kids still prefer corn dogs).

Experiential strategies are designed to help brands identify situations where prospects have open minds and then provide relevant experiences to form emotional and physical connections. A funny commercial or sleek banner ad cannot replicate the experience of handing a person a product or directly showing them the power of new technology. Without a doubt, no strategy succeeds as frequently as experiential marketing.

Samples and Keepsakes and Discounts, Oh My!

Sam's Club and Costco get it. When I visit a warehouse club, it's about so much more than stocking up on paper towels — it's snack time.

A trip to Sam's Club is a journey through the world's largest tasting menu. It's an opportunity to enjoy a gourmet nine-course meal of pretzels and cheesecake bites. These stores are littered with sample carts manned by service reps offering everything from chips and salsa to lasagna. When I go to Sam's, I walk around with an open mind to experience new products. As a result, I routinely buy products that aren't on my list.

Not every salesperson offers treats, though. Some hawk cell phone plans and cable subscriptions (far less appetizing). The next time you visit one of these stores, sit back for a few minutes and compare the traffic between the person offering food and the person pitching a new cellular plan. Shoppers won't touch that person with a 20-foot pole, but they make a beeline to the friendly person holding a plate of cheese cubes.

This stark contrast should tell you everything you need to know about the effectiveness of samples versus sales pitches. First, enrolling in a cable plan at a grocery store lacks relevance and context. On the other hand, snagging a cup of spiced apple cider makes sense because consumers already are prepared to purchase food items. Shoppers who take the free sample appreciate the gift, and they are far more likely to purchase the item than if they had simply walked past its packaging (assuming they enjoyed the sample).

How many times have you been shopping for food and found yourself upset about the prospect of a free sample? I'd guess not many. Unless you were on a diet at the time, you likely took the little plastic cup with a smile and went about your business.

This happened when we worked with Snapple on a cross-country tour to promote the brand's Straight Up Tea. We approached target consumers in places where they might be thirsty for something new. With 19 branded vehicles stocked with product, we traveled to 27 major cities and surprised customers at parks, 5K runs, festivals, farmers markets, and other places where Snapple drinks could be engaged. We handed out more than *half a million bottles* of ice-cold tea to parched customers across the country.

Even individuals who thought they might not like Straight Up Tea were happy to accept a free sample and at least give it a try. It was uplifting to see people who had written off the Snapple brand give it another shot. The tea wasn't an immediate hit with everyone, but the vast majority of people enjoyed the drink. This seemingly minor interaction opened the door to possible future Snapple purchases. Impressed consumers were likely to tell their friends about the free drink; if those friends were Snapple naysayers, the recent converts might say, "I used to feel the same way, but then I gave this new tea a try."

The Snapple brand team undoubtedly had a variety of tactics and strategies it could have implemented for this new product introduction.

They wisely leaned on experiential marketing, breaking into 27 local markets and uncovering the undeniable value of passing out a substantial amount of samples.

> *Getting our new line of products in the mouths of our core demo was an integral part of our product launch. We needed a partner with national reach, value, experience, and tactical agility! To hand out over 500,000 bottles throughout the U.S. in such a short time provided the reach we were looking to achieve. Obviously, we're very happy with the results.*
>
> *—Dr Pepper Snapple Group*

For brands that have products to hand out, sampling programs provide easy and effective opportunities to win new customers. But what about companies with larger products? And what about B2B organizations with more complex services? It's not exactly easy to hand out a sample of IT infrastructure security or backup power sources for data centers.

Fortunately, even brands that sell machinery or expensive software can engage with prospects through in-person experiences. Coupons, swag, live demos, and trade show tours — which we will cover in Chapter 3 — all provide for memorable experiential marketing activations.

At events for telecommunications company ZTE, for example, we hosted interactive trivia games to boost audience interest in the company's new smartphones. Our brand ambassadors presented fun facts about the devices and then challenged participants to a little test. If participants passed the test, they received a ZTE coupon. People who didn't know the answers got a little help until they got it right. This ensured everyone left with ZTE swag and a favorable impression of the brand. Those who took the test felt a little smarter, stood a little taller, and walked away with new knowledge of a phone brand they might not have considered before.

The test provided a fun environment to educate people on the technical differentiators of ZTE products without making it feel like a chore. By turning the pitch into a game, we were able to promote major selling points — such as the Apple-equal processor, the best camera in the industry, and the much lower price point — and tell a story without sounding like salespeople.

When games and live experiences don't fit the environment, old-fashioned swag is the best way to go. Good swag — from hats and t-shirts to more unusual offerings like selfie sticks and phone chargers — creates a physical and emotional connection to a brand that keeps positive impressions alive long after the event ends. Swag that resonates with both the personality of the brand and the needs of the audience builds an experience worth the investment. According to the British Promotional Merchandise Association[9], 87 percent of event attendees keep the swag they receive for at least one year; 79 percent of attendees who receive swag say they would consider purchasing products from the associated company in the future.

Conference knickknacks often gain a bad reputation because companies haphazardly slap logos on cheap items like plastic pens and call them branded swag. *Useful* swag, however, stands out because it serves a purpose. Small logos should be friendly reminders of the brand that provided the swag rather than the driving force behind a giveaway.

Not all swag is created equal, though. What you give away needs to tie back to your audience, message, and expected outcome. Backstage passes to concerts count as swag, but you would quickly run out of money if you gave those out at every conference. The most value-driven giveaways fulfill attendee needs while reminding them of a brand's products and services.

The key is matching the brand message and value to the item. A company that boasts about how its software solutions save time should not give away time-wasting items like fidget spinners; it should instead focus on something practical and efficient, such as a pocket planner or a Swiss Army knife. For a brand focused on the outdoors, meanwhile, it would make perfect sense to offer bottled water, sunscreen, or sunglasses. The more useful the gift, the more likely the customer will keep it — and the longer your brand's message will live in their office or home.

Bringing Your Product to Life

We all make impulse purchases. Those of us who lived through the heyday of TV infomercials remember just how convincing some of this programming could be.

I'm a little embarrassed to admit it, but I once found myself drawn to a presentation on QVC. I was flipping through the channels when I suddenly saw a beautiful bouquet of tulips. The vibrant colors caught my eye, and — ignoring the quizzical look from my wife — I watched the presentation from beginning to end. When the two personable saleswomen told me how to order, I picked up the phone and did just that.

Naturally, my enthusiasm for the purchase waned during the "six to eight weeks required for processing and handling." When the package of tulip bulbs arrived, I placed them in the basement and assured myself I would get around to planting them soon. As fate would have it, they remained untouched in my dark basement for several weeks. One day, I went downstairs and saw something incredible: The tulips, unplanted and away from sunlight, were growing!

At that moment, I saw the beauty of the flowers I ordered all those weeks ago. I laughed and thought, "If they can grow here, I bet they can grow in the dirt." And they did. They grow every year in my backyard, serving as a living reminder of the excitement I felt when I first saw the presentation on QVC.

In my defense, I'm not the only person who has kept QVC on the air. This interactive shopping network operates all over the world, boasting $8.7 billion in net annual sales with 15 channels, seven websites, and more than a billion online visitors in 2016.[10]

How do QVC and other shopping channels succeed where commercials fail? They don't stop at 30-second sales pitches; they demonstrate products in real time. People get to see how products work, how to use them, and why the purchase is worth the money. QVC basically is a series of how-to videos on products you never knew you needed. The countdown timer in the corner adds a slight sense of urgency that some shoppers need to take the leap. These presentations follow a specific scientific formula that shopping channels have perfected over the years to maximize orders.

The younger generation might scoff at how older people pay attention to these shows, but they do the same thing — just on a different platform. YouTube unboxing videos are among the most popular pieces of content on the internet.[11] For several minutes at a time, viewers watch as other people take new products out of their boxes and discuss every component they uncover in the process. Millions of viewers sit enraptured while internet strangers explore their new toys for the first time.

My 19-year-old son, Stephen, enjoys a subcategory of this genre. He loves to browse YouTube for supercar videos, which mostly involve a person with an iPhone sitting behind the exhaust port while someone else revs the engine. I've never driven a Bugatti Veyron, but my son's enthusiasm for this subgenre of videos means I could probably tell you exactly what one sounds like. These videos have only increased my son's desire to experience the real thing, but he'll have to wait until he becomes a professional baseball player or successful businessman to afford it.

The rise of virtual reality and augmented reality makes these types of videos even more engaging. It's one thing for consumers to watch a two-dimensional video of a product, but it's a new experience altogether to launch into the world of the product and interact with a digital replica in a scalable, highly immersive environment.

For example, Star Wars and Google teamed up for the release of "The Last Jedi" by creating AR stickers of R2-D2, Stormtroopers, and more that users can insert into photos. Although this technology is still in its infancy, VR experiences are popping up all over the internet and at live events around the world. As this technology becomes cheaper, brands will have more opportunities to maximize audience engagement through sophisticated digital experiences.

We'll cover some interesting uses for AR later, but let's stick to VR for now. The difference between the two realities is subtle but significant: VR takes users to a whole new world, and AR enhances the world around them.

For brands like GoPro and Red Bull, which promote more of a lifestyle than a product, VR is a natural fit. People associate GoPro with outdoor exploration and adventure, and Red Bull evokes the can-do attitude of achievement through action. You don't need to touch GoPro's newest product to develop an emotional connection with it — you just need to sit through the high-octane, first-person VR experience of a person who went cliff diving with one strapped to his head.

These types of VR experiences are great, but they aren't the perfect fit for everyone. Some people cannot put on the equipment without feeling nauseated, and no brand wants to be associated with losing your lunch — particularly those working in consumables.

Each of these marketing channels (QVC, YouTube, and VR experiences) is compelling and deserving of a spot in the library of marketing strategies. But even with this wealth of tools, something's missing. These techniques bring customers closer to the products than sales pitches or commercials, but people universally prefer a real-life experience to the mirage that digital media provides. In other words, they are great tactical choices to leverage within a smart experiential strategy.

In the booming age of online shopping, you might be surprised to learn that a 2017 eMarketer study[12] revealed that most American consumers still prefer to buy nearly every category of product in person rather than online. In addition to seeing and hearing about a product, being able to touch and smell that same product helps individuals create more powerful memories and stronger associations with the brands behind the experiences.

The more senses a product is able to engage, the stronger a consumer impression becomes. During memory formation, people rely partially on the same regions of the brain[13] that receive messages from their five senses. By triggering more of those senses, experiential marketers create powerful connections in the minds of their target audiences.

This truth doesn't apply solely to products with pleasant smells or physical forms, though. When someone interacts with a product in person or plays with a live demo, everything contributes to the experience. The sight of the product or computer hosting the demo; the smell of the room and the detergent on a shirt; the sounds of a representative guiding the experience; and the feel of the product, computer mouse, or other interactive components all combine to form full-sensory moments that create memorable experiences.

When those senses all pull in the same direction, the experience becomes even more impactful. For example, if a software company named Cupcake Software Solutions were to host a fun demo where people receive cupcakes and use computers adorned with sprinkles, consumers would likely remember that experience for life. However, if a company presents conflicting sensory information — a vegan bakery showcasing its latest offerings while the smell of bacon is in the air — the sensory synergy will lose its effect.

Experiential marketing combines the power of sensory information with effective brand presentations to create positive, lasting impressions in the minds of consumers. Think of it like a fortune cookie: You can break it with your fingers, hear the crunch as you split the pieces, smell the aroma, taste the sweet flavor, and see the message on the piece of paper hidden inside. These full-sensory experiences exponentially magnify the power of marketing events, increasing the likelihood that a consumer will flip from asking, "Why would I want this?" to exclaiming, "I have to have this!"

Induce an "A-ha" Moment

The transition from a consumer wondering whether they want something to realizing they *need* it is a driving reason experiential marketing works so well. When it's time to educate consumers about what a product does and why it's relevant to them, that moment of enlightenment is key to the success of the interaction. The best — and perhaps only — way to create that special moment is to bring your product to life in a fully immersive way.

Watching these transformative moments is one of the best parts of my job. One of our clients, Fiskars, sells tree pruners. People who use tree pruners know the frustration of cutting branches multiple times, using a modified sawing motion to hack through a sea of small sticks. When they use a Fiskars product and feel how effortlessly it slices through the wood, their eyes light up. No commercial, pop-up ad, VR experience, or in-store display can replicate that moment when the customer realizes, "A-ha! I get it. I need this!"

My car-loving son is enamored with his preferred brand of car, but he has yet to experience the real thing. After struggling to close sales with people like him, BMW figured that more customers would buy its cars if they could sit behind the wheel. In 2014, the German automaker invited some of its target consumers to take a new sports car for a test drive.[14]

These people might have seen videos of the cars online, but they hadn't felt their heads whip back as they accelerated from zero to 60 mph. They had seen clips of the throaty exhaust, but they hadn't smelled it for themselves. The results were predictably successful: One in four people who attended the test drive bought a new car after the demonstration.

Regardless of how amazing a product looks in an advertisement, nothing beats experiencing the real thing. Most consumers hesitate to pull out their wallets based on secondhand information, but that hesitation fades away in favor of excitement when a brand creates a one-to-one connection between a user and a product.

People want to drive the car. They want to drink the tea, sample the yogurt, and win the trivia game. Trying before you buy relieves fears through personal tests and forms emotional bonds that can last a lifetime. Brands have a golden opportunity to provide the experiences their audiences crave, but they must first acknowledge the limitations of indirect forms of marketing and make in-person experiences a priority.

A fun learning experience and "A-ha" moment removes the grimy feel of advertising and replaces it with authentic engagement. Experiential marketing enables you to reach customers in environments where they are amenable to learn and actively interested in what you have to offer. That explains why after an experience, 94 percent of consumers have a better chance of recalling your brand.[15]

CHAPTER 2

Go Where the Ducks Are

"We need to stop interrupting what people are interested in and be what people are interested in."
—*Craig Davis, former chief creative officer, J. Walter Thompson*

Imagine today is your first time duck hunting. You have all the necessary gear, including camouflage clothing and a duck call (which you bought on QVC because the salesman made the device sound just like an excited duck). You figured it would be a long day, so you packed a lunch full of the snacks you bought based on the samples you enjoyed at Sam's Club.

With your preparations complete, you climb in your new BMW and drive up into the mountains. You set up camp, blow into your duck call, and wait for the perfect opportunity. After what feels like hours, some prey wanders into your view. You take careful aim at your target and pull the trigger. Direct hit!

Unfortunately, the bear you shot turns around and eats you. Whoops. Hunting for ducks at 12,000 feet might seem well and good, but it's a bit like shopping for shoes at the farmers market — you're in the wrong environment.

Marketing, like duck hunting, requires a lot more than the right tools. Marketers must use those tools in the right context and target audiences in their natural habitats. That's why I like to say, "If you want to hunt ducks, go where the ducks are."

Most marketers understand this concept in the digital environment. Facebook makes it easy to target people by factors ranging from location to employment status to political views. Ad services promise to do the same by putting messages in front of the people most receptive to your content. But as I noted in the first chapter of this book, consumer interaction with online advertising is limited at best — and online targeting often feels more like harassment than a legitimate response to expressed interest.

Say your father-in-law wanted a pair of loafers for his birthday. You generically searched "best loafers" on Google, looked at a few pairs, and then gave up and bought him a Bass Pro Shop gift card. Unknowingly, you made the fatal error of telling the internet you might want some loafers.

Suddenly, loafers are stalking you across the internet. These seemingly innocent shoes are more aggressive than an ex-boyfriend snooping on your friends' social media feeds to see what you have been doing. They follow you around Facebook. They appear next to articles on your favorite news sites. They pop up on your Instagram feed and in the pre-roll ads of YouTube videos.

Everywhere you go online, the loafers follow. Weary after a long day of avoiding banner ads, you finally turn the lights off to get some sleep. A flicker of light causes you to bolt upright in bed. Have the loafers crept into your bedroom to claim your credit card? Yes, actually. Amazon just sent you a push notification about a sale on loafers.

It might sound like the plot of a cheesy B-movie, but this is the reality of digital targeting. Advertisers call it "personalization," but it's really just bots acting like they know what you want. Brands examine your previous behavior and nestle themselves into your browsing experience, hoping you'll accidentally click one of their banner ads and make a purchase. And even if you finally do become a customer, they reciprocate by sending you even more ads. The bots think, "If this person wanted one pair of loafers, he or she definitely wants another pair *now!*"

In theory, online targeting makes sense. It's extremely inexpensive, and brands can use it to reach people who have expressed interest in their products. Although this is mildly better than advertising to the general population, online targeting doesn't win by a wide margin. Research shows that targeted digital ads fail to deliver on the expectations they promise. In 2017, the click-through rate of display ads online was a measly 0.05 percent.[16] That's five clicks per 10,000 impressions, many of which were likely accidents.

How many other marketing strategies can get away with a success rate that low? Plus, the rise of ad-blocking software[17] simultaneously shows consumers fewer ads while ensuring the ones that do slip through feel even more intrusive. Even relevant online ads are met with incredulous outbursts of, "How did this get past the filter?"

Paying for targeted ads might seem inexpensive, but wasted money is wasted money regardless of how much you spend. Why throw a few dollars in the trash when you could use that money to pay for part of something more useful? How about an experience that doesn't remind consumers of being haunted by a pair of shoes?

This is especially true when the consumers who do see your ads end up more annoyed than interested. By the time the loafers leave you alone, you might be so traumatized by the experience that you become an advocate of formal sandals.

Customers have turned to ad-blocking software because they're tired of ads — and who could blame them? Their online lives are cluttered beyond repair, filled with more marketing material than useful content. Some estimates[18] say consumers are exposed to more than 11,000 targeted advertisements every month! I don't know about you, but I would struggle to name 11,000 products (let alone afford them). Pair this unwelcome surge of advertising with the shrinking human attention span — which is now shorter than that of a goldfish[19] — and it's easy to see how online ads earned their less-than-stellar reputation.

None of this is to say that you should stop fine-tuning these targeted ads, though. Take the time to recognize these ads for what they are, but understand that there are other marketing approaches that can engage audiences in more impactful ways. And don't forget to use your customer data on more memorable techniques with higher ROI — like experiential marketing.

Targeting Done Right

Experiences trump ads every time. Even in an environment where people are open to advertisements, consumers would much rather enjoy a no-pressure experience than listen to a sales pitch. Think about it: You are more likely to engage parents at the park with a free sample of a snack than risking the chance of them skipping your commercial for the same product.

The best experiential marketing campaigns meet target consumers where they live, work, play, or shop — locations where they are comfortable and open to new information. Rather than disrupting customer routines, experiences should augment their lives through unobtrusive, optional, and appealing bonuses.

To target an experience, set up shop in a place that makes sense. If you offer noise-canceling headphones, for instance, visit music festivals, gadget conventions, and "loudest snoring" competitions. If you're peddling organic herbs and spices, hit the farmer's market circuit. Avoid offering milkshakes at the National Convention of Lactose Intolerance. If an environment is particularly busy, stand out from the crowd by making yourself the most attractive option available.

During these one-on-one branded experiences, customers can see exactly how a product fits into their lives and experience tangible benefits. They leave with positive impressions of the product and the brand, ideally taking away bits of swag or other physical reminders of how this product could enrich their lives.

My company works with Tractor Supply Company on an experiential program that takes place at state fairs across rural America. Although most people go to fairs to buy turkey legs bigger than their heads — not tractor parts, pet food, or farm tools — these fairs attract the company's target audience in a place where they're already having fun.

Families go on rides, play games, and make lasting memories. Through it all, Tractor Supply Company is right in the middle. We integrate ourselves into the fair with multifaceted experiences (which I'll discuss more later). We give away keepsakes, spread the good word about the brand's offerings, and add to the fun by creating games for kids and inviting others to enjoy the rural-lifestyle-themed environment. Participants often spend 30 minutes or more hanging out at the Tractor Supply Company Fair Tour experience, largely because the brand's presence makes sense in the fair environment. Our offerings add to the overall fair experience, and we don't make it feel as though we're constantly pushing a product or message.

After a family visits one of our exhibits, they wake up the next morning surrounded by reminders of the fun they had with Tractor Supply Company. They have trucker hats sporting the Tractor Supply Company logo hanging by the door, coupons on the counter to use at their local Tractor Supply company, and photos of the whole family having fun at the event on the fridge. They didn't buy anything, but they suddenly are immersed in the branding of the company.

With their new swag in tow, this family has the potential to become a word-of-mouth powerhouse for the brand. They post their family pictures on Facebook and Instagram, where they discuss the fun experience they enjoyed at the fair. Their friends comment on the post and share it with relatives, spreading one family's outing to an entire social network. For months, it's likely that this family will throw on branded hats when running errands and use the coupon book at their local Tractor Supply Company store — all while further promoting the brand's presence.

The beauty of the Fair Tour is that it allows us to really engage with our customers who know and love Tractor Supply Company and are loyal to us. The whole footprint of the event is intended to be a soft sell about what we offer and to overcome the hurdle of people thinking that Tractor Supply Company sells tractors — in reality, we sell everything but tractors.

We take what may be a traditional fair game and put a twist on it. A unique component of the tour is that we have vendor sponsors of the products that we sell in

> *our stores. This is a genuine way to weave them into the*
> *footprint.*
>
> —*Tractor Supply Company*

This type of word-of-mouth marketing is essential for any successful brand. Research from Nielsen[20] discovered that a recommendation from a friend is the most powerful form of advertising. Shockingly, people even trust the recommendations of people they've never met more than they trust branded content.[20] By using experiences and swag, you can plant the seeds of a word-of-mouth tidal wave that could someday spread far beyond your initial target audience.

In a dwindling retail environment where giants like Sears and J.C. Penney are struggling to make ends meet, this expansion[21] is a testament to the power of experiential marketing.

Last year, I was preparing to visit our Tractor Supply Company activation at the Minnesota State Fair. My daughter, Paige, insisted that I get a bucket of Sweet Martha's Cookies on my trip. I didn't have a clue what she was talking about, and I wondered how she heard about a random cookie company hundreds of miles away. As it turned out, her college roommate (a Minnesota native) was obsessed with these cookies.

After doing some research, I discovered the story of Martha and her cookies. Martha is a brilliant entrepreneur from Minnesota who is a living embodiment of "Go where the ducks are." She began in a small booth at the Minnesota State Fair in 1979. Thanks to her knack for business and keen skills in the kitchen, Martha quickly expanded her company into two small buildings that each housed more than six massive commercial ovens.[22]

Nearly 40 years later, Martha continues to maintain a major presence at the Minnesota State Fair. Her booths are more than sentimental reminders of her humble beginnings, though. Those booths move nearly 3 million cookies every day of the fair, with her team members and ovens working overtime during that span. In 2016, Sweet Martha's Cookies made a jaw-dropping $4 million over 12 days.[23]

What makes Sweet Martha's Cookies so special? For starters, the volume of cookies in a single order is absurdly large. When you get a literal bucket filled with four dozen of Martha's cookies — warm and fresh from the oven — it's impossible to put a lid on it. You're left with no other choice but to start eating the delicious treats right away.

The real kicker is Martha's location. She's located next to the fair's famous all-you-can-drink milk shop. Customers order their buckets of cookies and then grab a glass of classic milk, chocolate milk, soy milk, strawberry milk, and any other sort of milk that might go with cookies. The arrangement makes perfect sense: People go to the fair to forget their diets and have some fun. Milk and cookies fit right in with corn dogs, roller-coasters, and tractor pulls — and Martha's hometown roots certainly help.

As it turns out, my daughter knows several companies that go where the ducks are. She also let me know about Kendra Scott, a fashion and jewelry brand that found its experiential niche at large universities across the U.S.

In 2002, Kendra Scott's company made $1.7 million.[24] It wasn't a bad year, but it fell short of the explosive revenue she had envisioned. To kick-start her sales, Scott focused on sororities around the country and enlisted chapter members to act as her on-campus ambassadors. The brand gives its college ambassadors exclusive access to new items and limited-edition accessories, ensuring demand stays high while providing purchasers with a feeling of exclusivity. Scott's strategy worked like a charm, and her company now pulls in more than $200 million annually.

Kendra Scott has grown far beyond its status as a college-only brand, but the company still relies heavily on its influencers to drive sales. Members of the Kendra Scott campus influencer program get access to special events and exclusive products, acting as hosts at trunk shows where other college students can buy jewelry. Ambassadors do the marketing legwork within their sorority networks, building awareness and demand. In exchange for their work, they pocket a cut of the proceeds while the brand profits. The system works extremely well, thanks in large part to exclusive experiences that drive brand loyalty.

> *I think Kendra Scott's ambassador program works because most college women want the new, cute, and trendy jewelry and fashion. When you have representatives in your sorority you can turn to when you want to purchase a certain item from the brand, it's easy and makes sense. I'd rather buy a necklace this way because it's just my sorority sisters — I'm not dealing with a bunch of random people crowding into a store. We have the girls in my house that work for Kendra Scott, and it's much more personable to say, "Okay, I feel like I'm buying from this person instead of buying from a stranger."*
>
> *—Paige Randazzo*

These companies have perfected the art of experiential targeting. They don't try to shoehorn their brands into places that don't make sense — they find their customers and then take the show to them. Of course, these brands wouldn't be nearly as successful in their niches if their smart placement and good timing were not backed up by memorable experiences.

To ensure your perfect targeting doesn't go to waste, you must design an experience that rewards people who give you the gift of their attention.

Right Place, Right Time, Right Appearance

Even with great targeting, you still can't create the equivalent of a live-action banner ad if you don't provide the right experience. Your gut might tell you to find the busiest street corner in the world to showcase your brand. Your gut isn't necessarily wrong, but it's overlooking the fact that this crowded location is worthless without the right timing, the right appearance, and relevant messaging. Marketers assume that more people equate to more engagement, but suboptimal environments create the risk of people ignoring your experiences — or worse, viewing you as a nuisance.

Imagine it's game day at Lambeau Field. You are en route to what is certain to be an exciting clash between the Green Bay Packers and their bitter rivals, the Chicago Bears. After a challenging commute and a frustrating search for parking, kickoff is only 20 minutes away. As you speed walk to the stadium entrance, a man steps out of nowhere and asks, "Would you like to come inside this trailer to see an interactive exhibit of Brett Favre's incredible career?"

Truth be told, you normally would have jumped at the opportunity to reflect on the legendary quarterback's career. But in this case, the timing couldn't be worse.

Is this experience even worth your time? With a Favre jersey already on your back and three signed footballs at home, it seems like an appealing proposition. Even though the exhibit aligns with your interests in a convenient location, it's hard to see the immediate value the experience would bring to your life. Instead of a fellow fan, the exhibit rep feels more like an obstacle between you the stadium. You smile, politely decline the human pop-up ad's offer, and make a beeline to your seat — forgetting all about the potential experience.

To avoid creating a similarly misplaced opportunity through your marketing efforts, go to venues where passersby have the time and the desire to interact. People expect personalized advertising regardless of the situation. That doesn't mean you need to know their names beforehand, but consumers will be unimpressed if you offer something that doesn't fit seamlessly into their current activities and personal interests.

During this theoretical trip to Lambeau Field, the Favre experience nailed the first step (right place) but flunked the next two (right time, right appearance).

For starters, there's a big difference between targeting tailgaters three hours before the game and trying to engage fans who are rushing to get to their seats. When you set up in a place where people have time to kill, swing for the fences. Build a large, immersive experience where they can leisurely interact with the environment.

If you absolutely must target people who are in a rush, make it snappy. Quickly hand out samples or swag, allowing them to get the full experience without breaking stride. People entering a cold stadium probably won't want to stop and chat with a brand ambassador, but they might happily take some branded hand warmers or a thermos full of hot chocolate. Give consumers something of value to use either immediately or at home, but don't disrupt their day to make an exchange.

Design your event to look professional. Starting at a young age, most of us learned to reject invitations from strangers (an unmarked white van doesn't help). Effective marketing allows participants to see what they're agreeing to before they commit. Label everything clearly and try to host your event in an open environment where the fun and games will naturally attract onlookers.

If the best way to lure in people is to place a brand ambassador outside to tell people, "Come in! It's fun! I promise!" you have already lost a significant chunk of your potential audience. Let the event speak for itself by creating a visually stimulating experience that draws a crowd. Once the first few brave souls give the experience a try, the rest will follow.

Our Tractor Supply Company activations use massive open entrances, ensuring people within 100 yards know they're headed to the Tractor Supply Company area. Everything is friendly, inviting, and free — a fact we make clear from the outset. At state fairs, where most booths want consumers to open their wallets, we pride ourselves on being a gratis oasis. People can enjoy exhibits and games suited for all ages, and everyone leaves with a smile, a bit of swag, and a few pictures. Best of all, nobody feels pressured — people are able to pace their experiences however they prefer.

Great experiences don't ask too much of their participants, and they don't seem out of place in their environments. Every event is different, but you can create positive memories and brand associations for your target audience by paying attention to context and designing an experience that matches.

Choose Your Own Adventure

Do you know why kids like to read "choose your own adventure" books? It's not because they enjoy getting eaten by a Yeti in the Himalayas. It's because of the freedom these books provide. They don't force a narrative on readers — they put audiences in the driver's seat and let them feel like they are steering the experience.

In that sense, adults aren't so different from children. We want to choose our own adventures, too. According to 2017 research from Oracle[25], consumers are more willing to embrace new technology when they feel in control of the experience. In addition, a psychological study from 2016[26] discovered that the desire to control situational outcomes creates a barrier between consumers and their acceptance of new products.

The research is clear: To get consumers to try new things, you must put them in control of their own experiences.

Digital ads take the opposite approach. They interrupt and derail the browsing experience by blocking access to the content consumers desire, holding people captive and forcing them to click the tiny red "x." It's frustrating, but companies continue to refer to this as "engagement." As far as I can tell, tricking people into clicking an advertisement doesn't qualify as a meaningful engagement (nor is it a good way to start a new relationship).

Done correctly, experiential activations provide consumers with exciting opportunities to choose their own adventures. The best ones create incentives to engage before stepping back and allowing participants to decide what that means for them. Customers feel empowered during these moments of discovery, opening their minds to learn about the brand and product behind the experience.

This involves creating *opt-in* experiences rather than *opt-out* ones. Don't kidnap people and force them to look for an exit — they will either storm off angrily or call the police, both of which can put a damper on an otherwise pleasant experiential campaign. Give participants full control, and don't try to stop them if they want to walk away. Even if you lose a few attendees, others will soon come along to take their places.

Long before Claritin was a household name, my marketing agency created a quick and effective awareness campaign for the brand that we hosted on the streets of a major city. We stood at busy street corners and asked pedestrians whether they suffered from seasonal allergies. Anyone could choose to ignore us or engage without skipping a beat. If they didn't have allergies, we simply said, "Great! Have a Claritin day!" If they stopped and said they had allergies, we gave them the full product experience. No one felt pressured. Everyone was free to choose whether to make eye contact, and the people who were interested received our full attention.

Part of letting participants choose their own adventure means eliminating step-by-step processes and replacing them with open exploration. We used to rely on a sequential model, which saw attendees take steps in a predetermined order. Years ago, we handed out passports and let people collect stamps. It sounded fun in theory, but people lost interest because we forced everyone to follow the same route at the same pace. For our marketers and participants alike, the experience felt more like herding livestock than facilitating fun and building rapport.

Since those early days, we have learned that consumers who guide their own experiences leave with more positive impressions than those who do not. It's one of the main reasons we offer eight different nonsequential activities at our Tractor Supply Company activations. Visitors can engage with all or none of them — we don't force people to take pictures on "Moose" the bull, but we make it look like so much fun that attendees want to climb on.

Sometimes, your KPIs mandate that you must give participants a gentle nudge in a certain direction. Phrases like "Hey, have you entered our sweepstakes yet?" encourage people to provide contact information without coming off as overly directive. Something like "Have you tried lassoing Pickles the pig today?" can generate interest and drive people to take more branded photos to post on social media. Let people explore at their own pace, but give a few gentle nudges along the way to help you gauge the success of the event.

With these tips, examples, and cautionary tales in mind, which would you rather be? The haunted loafers that stalk people across the internet or the brand that provides relevant, fun experiences for customers? Only one of these approaches captures the undivided attention of an audience for long stretches of time, educates people about products without becoming a sales pitch, and provides keepsakes and memories that last a lifetime.

Digital marketing isn't dead. Facebook, Instagram, and banner ads still have a time and a place. There's no need to eliminate your digital budget and fire your social media coordinator, but don't rely on these channels alone to spread the word about your brand. When it comes to enduring brand impressions and word-of-mouth promotion, experiential marketing takes the cake: 93 percent of consumers feel more of a connection to brands after experiences.[15]

CHAPTER 3

Provide a Professional Field Trip

"People shop and learn in a whole new way compared to just a few years ago, so marketers need to adapt or risk extinction." —Brian Halligan, co-founder and CEO, HubSpot

Remember what it felt like to wake up the morning of a school field trip?

You didn't beg your parents for five more minutes of sleep — you were downstairs and dressed before they finished their coffee. When you finally arrived at school, your friends were grinning ear to ear in the parking lot next to the bus. Everyone couldn't wait to do something new instead of sitting in the same old classroom and doing the same old math problems assigned by the same old teacher.

When my kids were in elementary school, students took an annual field trip around downtown St. Louis for a scavenger hunt. We split into groups — four kids to one adult — to explore the city and search for the buildings and landmarks they learned about in class. Students' eyes lit up with excitement every time they found themselves standing in front of buildings they had seen only in photos. On the bus ride back to school, students would take turns talking about their favorite discoveries from that day, describing specific features of each building, fountain, and steel arch that stood out in their minds and made each landmark memorable.

Field trips never feel like school, but they help kids learn just the same — maybe even better. They're a break from the monotony of day-to-day academics, and they certainly are memorable.

It's kind of a shame that field trips generally don't follow us into our professional lives. When was the last time your boss closed the office and chartered a bus to an exciting location for a day of learning that didn't quite feel like learning? Possibly never. Arranging an outing for an entire office (let alone just one department) is daunting — not to mention expensive.

Your brand, however, can offer its dream clients the type of field trip they've been waiting for: something convenient, highly memorable, and completely free of charge.

Take the Trade Show to the Decision Maker

Once upon a time, trade shows were the best field trips B2B decision makers could take. Clients, prospects, and vendors gathered in massive halls to attend presentations, visit booths, and talk shop — ideally scoring a few hot leads in the process. Every company worth its salt sent a contingency of high-level decision makers to relevant conferences because you had to put in your appearances if you wanted to make a name in any industry.

The major trade shows were like the Paris Fashion Week of their respective industries — with fewer expensive necklaces. If you wanted to rub shoulders with people who could make or break your sales goals with a handshake, you had to go. And why wouldn't you? At that time, the other option involved making cold calls from the comfort of your office. Even if your biggest industry conference happened to be the Wool Sweater Convention ... in Phoenix ... in the middle of July, it was better than spending another day flipping through your Rolodex while Toto played faintly in the background.

Decades later, Toto is no longer a radio staple. And trade shows? They have fallen out of favor with B2B bigwigs. In the final quarter of 2016, the B2B exhibition industry saw its first quarter of decelerated growth after 25 consecutive quarters of year-over-year expansion.[27] High-level decision makers no longer feel compelled to spend a week in Las Vegas cramming brochures into their briefcases.

Now that even Siegfried and Roy have left Vegas, what's even the point? You could catch a Celine Dion concert between seminars, but the trade show circuit isn't likely to recoup its former steam. In recent years, attendance has plummeted at some of the biggest shows for prominent B2B industries. Houston's Offshore Technology Conference experienced its third consecutive year of lower attendance in 2017.[28] Luxury brands at JCK Las Vegas (the jewelry industry's premier trade show) have noted a similar decline.[29] In Chicago, the Food Marketing Institute's well-known show shut down for good[30], citing its failure to achieve "the precise formula necessary for meeting today's industry needs."

According to a Frost and Sullivan survey from 2014, 79 percent of respondents believe traditional trade shows and conferences do not have enough decision makers in attendance.[31] This situation adds a degree of separation between sellers and buyers, which is the kiss of death in the B2B world. The precise formula that will save trade shows likely involves a ride in a DeLorean; like it or not, the time of trade shows has passed.

Companies that rely on trade shows for most of their B2B revenue are in trouble. These shows lack the staying power to provide a dependable source of leads. Trade show conference halls could soon be filled with interns on holiday, happy to work on their homework as salespeople desperately try to pitch them on new software. Not a pretty picture, is it?

Fortunately, there's a better option to embrace. This approach has been around since the glory years of the trade show, but it's massively underused. To truly make an impression, it's time to take things on the road.

The Beauty of B2B Mobile Roadshows

Why pitch to increasingly uninterested audiences at expensive trade shows when you could pull your booth into a prospect's parking lot and enjoy undivided attention? Given the dwindling attendance and effectiveness of trade shows, take a moment to consider which of the two following options sounds better:

Option 1: Spend a ton of money to set up a booth at a trade show. Hope that enough decision makers from one or two of your dream clients show up, notice your display, talk to your reps, and with excitement accept a pamphlet about your products. Pray against all odds that these decision makers remember the pamphlet, pull it out weeks later, rally the rest of the team, and set the wheels in motion to buy from you. As you finally make a sale, note that the devil has indeed pulled on his winter parka.

Option 2: Design a mobile tour, load your product into a vehicle of some sort, and visit every single company on your list of dream clients and prospects. Offer a fun, interactive, and immersive field trip for the entire office to capture each attendee's undivided attention for 30 minutes to an hour. Talk directly to multiple decision makers on their own turf, without your competitors lurking around the corner to downplay the value of your product or service. Bask in victory as a choir of angels descends upon your quarterly sales figures.

That might seem reductive, but the best choice is a no-brainer. Roadshows, as I outlined in the second option, offer everything trade shows wish they could provide.

Toward the end of the thriving trade show era, Hussmann (a B2B food services company) devoted a large percentage of its annual marketing budget to present at FMI Connect, the biggest trade show in its industry. Hussmann found itself adrift when FMI Connect shut down for good in 2016. The company had a new refrigeration system to promote, but it had no way to show potential buyers its product without the trade show. Hussmann team members could email pictures of the massive units, but it's a stretch to say many B2B buyers are swayed by still images of industrial refrigerators.

When Hussmann presented us with the problem, we offered the obvious solution: design a mobile tour that takes Hussmann's trade show presentation to its dream clients. With the go-ahead from Hussmann, we leased a 32-foot trailer, designed the experience to showcase Hussmann's history of innovation in its industry, loaded a refrigeration system into it, and hired two brand ambassadors to hitch a ride across the country. Before sending the tour on its way, Hussmann's marketing and sales team members reached out to current and potential customers to explain that the company wanted to show them a new product — and that the giant piece of machinery would travel straight to their doorsteps.

Unlike attending trade shows, prospects had nothing to lose. There was no need to fly to a trade show and pick up a pamphlet. Instead, the trailer sat in the company's parking lot and allowed employees to come and go as they pleased to see the system for themselves. Just about every company we contacted invited us to visit, and we set the wheels of the tour in motion.

From there, word-of-mouth began to spread at each corporate office. Anticipation heightened about the new refrigeration unit that would soon be in the parking lot. Stakeholders in every department — engineers, managers, operations, maintenance, and C-suite executives alike — shifted their schedules to ensure they would be in the office that day. Why? They knew something interesting was about to happen.

Similar to how no kid fakes illness on field trip day, no adult wants to miss the opportunity to experience something new while interrupting his or her typical work routine. After all, breaking up the monotony of meetings and spreadsheets to come outside — even for 30 minutes — and check out a cool piece of technology that could benefit your organization is a hard proposition to pass up.

To say prospects met us with excitement would be an understatement. At each location, we arrived by 6 a.m. to make sure the tents, signage, and trailer were all operational by the time the first employees pulled into the parking lot. We provided morning snacks and refreshments, and we treated our hosts to lunch as a way of thanking the visitors for spending time with us. Some people were so ready to see the exhibit that they came straight into the trailer from their cars. When was the last time your trade show booth created this type of engagement?

Once they were inside, we never made attendees feel like they were receiving a sales pitch or marketing campaign. To make the experience worthwhile, productive, and engaging, we knew we had to keep it educational. Attendees needed to understand why Hussmann created this innovative piece of technology: to help customers solve problems, curb maintenance-related issues, avoid inefficiencies, and reduce excessive costs. With our problem-solving motive at the forefront, attendees kept open minds and trusted us to walk them through the experience. We weren't salespeople in a booth trying to sneak brochures in their pockets; we were partners, working *together* to solve a problem unique to their company.

Our presentation focused on how the special features of Hussmann's refrigeration system could solve these companies' ongoing problems. After we made our introductory explanations, something magical happened: Attendees started to sell one another on the product, completely independent of our influence. They were in the midst of true "A-ha" moments.

Decision makers and influencers excitedly discussed how beneficial it would be to have these systems in every store, the money they would save, and how much easier maintenance would be. We provided the base experience to get everyone thinking, and the industry experts added their own knowledge to that foundation to fulfill the purpose we set out to achieve.

Everyone from the top executives and procurement positions to engineering technicians and maintenance staff spent a part of their day walking around the exhibit, talking with our brand ambassadors and Hussmann sale staff, and mulling over the potential benefits of adding these systems to their stores. Some days, more than 100 people would go through the trailer. Many of them would visit once, leave, and return with co-workers to talk about the experience together. By the time we left, prospects were more than halfway through the sales process, and none of them felt like they had been through a tedious sales call. We actually received praise from many locations, with potential customers thanking the Hussmann sales team for understanding their business needs.

> *The feedback we received from our customers was not only that the roadshow helped them make good decisions on the product line we focused on, but also that they appreciated the fact that we came directly to them. We showed them we know their time is valuable and that walking out of their office into our display was easy and a big reason we had so many decision makers and support staff experience it.*
>
> *The roadshow helped us to achieve the aggressive sales goals we had for this product line because we were able to get incremental sales from prospects who were not customers or who have not been customers for a while along with some key customers making commitments to this line. Intuitively, we know we have to continue to find creative ways to get in front of our customers and prospects, and the roadshow strategy delivers.*
>
> *—Hussmann*

Think back to the past two chapters. In the first, we talked about the importance of meeting prospects in a comfortable environment and engaging all five senses during an experience. In the second, we discussed the importance of going where the ducks are and letting people choose their own adventure. B2B mobile trade show tours check both boxes by bringing an immersive experience straight to the doorstep of your customers, allowing you to step back and take the role of a guide as customers experience the magic for themselves.

Executives at Hussmann told me this experience provided much more bang for their buck. By taking the field trip to the prospects, we created a more strategic campaign with a higher ROI. Before the tour was over, Hussmann already had received orders for hundreds of thousands of dollars of this unit. When was the last time you got a tangible, transparent ROI from a trade show before it was over?

Supplementing Your Field Sales

To the uninitiated, mobile trade show tours might sound suspiciously like field sales. In truth, they are complementary pieces of an effective sales strategy, with mobile trade show tours creating the sparks that salespeople need.

The typical pitch feels more like a meeting than an experience. Most involve briefcases, pamphlets, business cards, and catered lunches. Few are more memorable than any other meeting — once you've seen a few thousand PowerPoint presentations, you've seen them all.

Like mobile trade show tours, sales reps visit potential clients on their turf. That's a huge plus, but decision makers rarely clear their calendars to ensure they are in the office when sales reps come calling. After sitting through the same emotionless spiel several times a year, B2B buyers become bored and less likely to become customers. Field reps try their best, but many of the decision makers I've spoken with use these pitch meetings as opportunities to catch up on the hundreds of emails they receive each day.

None of these limiting factors should cause you to fire your field sales team, of course. Many sales reps are good at what they do, and the ones who subvert client expectations can transform mundane meetings into experiences of their own. This age-old tactic still has its uses, but you shouldn't hang your hat on less-effective techniques when mobile trade show tours and other experiential options are on the table.

One of our clients, a medical equipment company called Invacare, prides itself on the effectiveness of its mobile sales teams. The first time I spoke with Rod Mills, the company's rehab sales and marketing manager, he went out of his way to tell me that he thought the person who hired us was wasting the company's money. Ouch!

> *I've been with Invacare for 23 years, and we've done these field promotion programs in the past where we managed them internally. I'm very conservative with Invacare's money, and there was some initial sticker shock. My original hesitancy was that it was going to cost us a lot of money, and I wasn't sure that we couldn't do it ourselves.*
>
> *I was crazy for thinking we could do it on our own because it ended up being such a better program. We got deeper coverage and put way more eyes on our products than we would've been able to. The investment versus what we got was certainly there — I just didn't see it in the beginning.*
>
> *—Invacare*

Initially, Invacare thought it could handle this program in-house. Once its team realized the numerous moving parts that were required to push this mobile tour into action, Invacare turned to us for the heavy lifting. We developed and activated a mobile tour to promote a new state-of-the-art line of motorized wheelchairs. Customers liked the products, and the sales team was moving units quickly — but the company saw opportunities for even greater success.

By the time we finished our mobile tour, we managed to make Rod a believer. As it turns out, even a seasoned veteran of outside sales can appreciate the power of an effective new marketing campaign.

To start, Invacare needed to demonstrate why its wheelchairs were leagues above other models on the market. Our team filled four vans with several of Invacare's wheelchairs and followed the same proprietary playbook we used when we promoted Hussmann's refrigeration systems. After reaching out to numerous hospitals, doctor's offices, and physical therapy clinics, we took our show on the road. In the first year of our campaign, we secured spaces in local hotel conference rooms, which drew large crowds but lacked intimacy. In the second year, we embraced our mobility and brought Invacare's products directly to customers' offices.

In addition to our core team, Invacare's staff and a few local brand advocates were on hand for this mobile tour. These real-life customers could speak about the life-changing benefits of the chairs. The individuals added a new layer to the experience, speaking earnestly to decision makers about how Invacare's chairs were more durable, more reliable, and better engineered than other products on the market.

I can recall vividly the time one brand advocate shared his story with a group of physical therapists. After a car accident left him paralyzed, this man had lain in bed for five years because he couldn't fathom how to navigate life in a motorized wheelchair. Every time he tried, he immediately returned to his bed in agonized frustration.

One day, this man tried using the new chair from Invacare. For the first time in half a decade, he felt a renewed ability to enjoy life. He started going out to concerts and restaurants, navigating crowds with ease long after he had resigned himself to a life of solitude. His story resonated with everyone in a way that no pitch from a salesperson (or even a video interview) could.

After listening to testimonials and learning about the value each Invacare chair provided for users, we then invited attendees to test out Invacare's chairs by navigating an obstacle course. Medical practitioners maneuvered around each other in both Invacare chairs and competitor products, with Invacare chairs winning out by a wide margin every time. Those who used the competitors' products routinely felt unstable or unsafe as they attempted to navigate impromptu lanes of cones, bumps, and ramps — individuals using Invacare chairs glided through with ease.

Talk about a true "A-ha" moment! No brochure or PowerPoint presentation could have accomplished what we achieved with that mobile tour. After 30 seconds in a chair, we had decision makers lining up to contact Invacare about pricing and order quantities.

Today, Rod Mills is one of our biggest advocates. He experienced how the mobile tour created a level of emotional engagement and hands-on participation that no traditional sales meeting could match. I still get chills when I think about the power of this particular mobile tour, and I suspect Rod feels the same way.

We look forward to many more years of working with the Invacare team. This company truly is changing lives, and we are grateful to be part of that mission.

The Past, Present, and Future of Mobile Roadshows

As the trade show industry continues to lose steam, B2B buyers still need to see, feel, and touch new products and services. Mobile Roadshows provide this solution across any industry or product line, and more brands are making way for these tours in their budget. In a 2019 study, around two-thirds of brand-side B2B marketers said they expected event and experiential marketing budgets to increase over the next year and a half (this represents a 17 percent increase over the previous year). Respondents expected an average of 24 percent growth in these areas of their budgets.[32]

While higher-ups abandon trade shows in droves — opting to stay home and let lower-level team members deal with flight delays and cramped conference centers — mobile trade show tours place products directly in front of the people who support the decision makers. This ultimately speeds up the decision-making process and fosters loyalty after a sale.

Field sales teams still have their place — people always have questions, and personal relationships remain a vital component of a comprehensive sales strategy long after the mobile tour is over. In turn, salespeople are looking for more productive tools to help customers and other prospects along in the sales process. Simply put, some products just look better in person than on paper; and the ones that boast impressive ROI generation often must be seen to be believed.

However, mobile tours increasingly drive better results than other channels. They also provide an incredible opportunity to build upon current customer relationships. We loaded our trailer with a refrigeration system that allowed guests to see it, touch it, open the doors, and understand how easy it was to maintain. We used VR to show what the line of refrigerated cases would look like in a store.

We took a similar approach with a new B2B client, Vertiv. Its unique industrial products – thermal units that cool data processing centers and backup redundancy power units that bring power back online within nanoseconds – are far too big to fit into touring vehicles. Similar to

Invacare, Vertiv originally thought it could execute this huge mobile tour on its own, but it quickly realized it needed an agency to help activate and manage the campaign – this is where we stepped in

Office workers, managers, decision makers, and even CEOs would love to take the occasional field trip. If you close your eyes, you can almost see them: executives sitting in stuffy boardrooms, sneaking glances out the window and wondering when the bus will arrive.

Each time we visit an office, prospects are thrilled to be engaged away from their desks. It's an interesting phenomenon. Mobile trade show tours never feel like stale meetings or sales calls. They are always well-attended, and you can usually feel the buzz of energy in the room. Prospects don't have to travel away from their families and sleep in an uncomfortable hotel room while wishing they weren't on a business trip. Instead, they're having fun and cannot wait to tell their friends and families, "You won't believe what I got to do at work today!"

Looking ahead, it's exciting to consider the ways that emerging technology will make mobile trade show tours even better — particularly for B2B brands selling difficult-to-represent products like software services, large machinery, and technical offerings.

AR and VR will soon transform mobile trade show tours into even more immersive experiences. Consider our refrigeration tour with Hussmann. We loaded our trailer with a refrigeration system that represented the full product, but it lacked some of the physical components that showcased key product features. To make up for the missing pieces, we used VR to show what a line of refrigerated cases would look like in a store. In this curated environment, customers could see the product in a new, engaging way.

By equipping two trucks with VR technology, customers all over the country were able to experience industrial-sized products in new ways. Two different stations of headsets and touchscreens allowed viewers to immerse themselves in the product's inner workings — such as examining the inside of one of the refrigeration units' fans — all while learning about its mechanics.

> *One of our goals was not to have products in the trucks. We had a roadshow a few years ago with a couple products but it was too limiting. This roadshow focused on several product lines, so we needed the convenience of touch screen monitors that became interactive brochures. The experience was broader in product scope. The Tour staff was amazing at coaching our local teams on how the event was going to run, everyone's roles, and key learning from past events.*
>
> *The feedback we received from our distributors was they got to see customers and prospects they rarely get to see along with regular customers. It truly was a win-win.*
> *—Vertiv*

Imagine the results if we were to repeat this tour with AR technology included. We could hand iPads to attendees as they entered the trailer and encourage them to view the system through our AR app as a brand ambassador walked them through key features. For instance, when a brand ambassador opened a hatch that normally houses the system's state-of-the-art motor, participants could point their tablets toward the area and see a rendering of the motor. When a rep pointed out the system's impeccable cooling capabilities, attendees could watch the glass doors frost over through their AR devices. The possibilities are limitless, and the rapid advancement of AR and VR technology means exhibits like this are closer than they seem — they already exist.

Even without augmented experiences, mobile tours remain the premier option for brands in every industry — especially B2B — to increase engagement with their most coveted potential customers. They also offer an unmatched opportunity to turn tryers into buyers with transparent ROI metrics. These experiences deliver big results, exponentially increasing ROI by beating other marketing campaigns at both ends of the budget spectrum. In the 2019 study mentioned earlier, three-fourths of brand-side B2B marketers also noted that among their brand's marketing tactics, experiential is the most successful (that's a 14 percent increase from 2018).[32]

By offering hands-on experiences to key decision makers through mobile trade show tours, brands can stand out from the competition, halve their sales cycles, and double their pipelines — simply by giving decision makers and their support teams an excuse to take a brief field trip.

PART II
ENGAGE

CHAPTER 4

Activate Your Brand

"I've learned that people will forget what you said, people will forget what you did, but people will never forget how you made them feel." —Maya Angelou

I was thrilled when my daughter decided to stay in Missouri for college. I initially thought she would try to get as far away from her family as possible (like so many other teenagers), but I felt incredibly lucky when she chose to attend the University of Missouri.

Instead of flying her home for the holidays and missing her the rest of the year, I'm able to drop by for big sporting events, to attend "Dad's Weekend" at her sorority, or just to grab a coffee and catch up. It's nice to have an excuse to get out of town, and Columbia is a great college town for a fun weekend away.

From our front door to her dorm room, the trip to the university takes less than two hours. That might sound easy, but the drive likely is the most boring stretch of highway in the continental U.S. There's no scenery, no cute shops, and no world's biggest anything — nothing but the quintessential Midwestern landscape of flat fields as far as the eye can see. There's a jolt of excitement when I get to drive on a hill, which certainly qualifies as entertainment when you're trapped in a car in Nowhere, Missouri. It's good old-fashioned rural America at its finest.

The only respite from the open road is the hundreds of billboards that dot the highway. Rather than entertain weary road warriors, however, the massive signs blend into the drab monotony of the experience. No one pays much attention to these archaic ads, but that doesn't stop fast-food chains, motels, mom-and-pop shops, and faraway tourist attractions from sinking thousands of dollars every month into these mute giants of advertising.

Billboards embody the low-risk status quo. No marketer will get in trouble with a higher-up for purchasing space on a highway billboard. It's a safe commodity — and almost entirely pointless.

I've made that drive countless times at this point. Of the hundreds of billboards that line Interstate 70 between St. Louis and Columbia, there is only one (well, technically seven) that could be considered "engaging."

If you visit Columbia for a fun weekend of SEC football before heading to St. Louis, you can enjoy these special billboards. Get on the eastbound highway and drive for about 20 minutes. You'll come across six billboards in rapid succession, each emblazoned with a single, large letter. Put together, they spell out M-I-Z-Z-O-U, a friendly reminder of the fine institution in your rearview mirror.

These billboards might cost the University of Missouri six times more than a single one, but this combination is more than six times as effective. Mizzou managed to turn a tired form of advertising into something at least *mildly* memorable. Kudos to the university, but those advertising dollars ended up helping the buyer of the seventh billboard even more.

The six billboards spelling out M-I-Z-Z-O-U used to stand proud and uninterrupted, but I spotted something new on a recent drive back to St. Louis. In front of the familiar series of six billboards stood a new sign with a simple message: "Straight to the Point: University of Missouri – St. Louis."

In one clever move, the university system's campus in St. Louis found a golden opportunity to swoop in and steal the show — a brilliant technique we'll cover in detail in Chapter 6. Suddenly, the following six billboards didn't feel as significant. They shrank in the shadow of the new billboard that turned an otherwise boring stretch of highway into an amusing competitive jab. Unfortunately, with 20 minutes down and about another hour and 40 minutes to go, the joy of seeing that clever billboard faded quickly.

The other billboards along the way are far less memorable. Unless you're in immediate need of some food or gas and cannot stand the thought of driving a few extra miles to civilization, you can safely ignore the rest of these outdated ads.

Flat Ads Are Forgettable Ads

There's nothing more passive than flat advertising. When brands insert themselves into reading materials, billboards, and even television shows, they do so in the vain hope that people will stop what they're doing to listen to a sales pitch. It's almost like subliminal messaging. These advertisers imagine that consumers will subconsciously absorb their logos and categorize them as a "good brand" the next time they go to make a purchase.

Is this a successful approach? Does it engage consumers? Can any brand hang its hat on passive marketing and expect to boost sales? If the drive between St. Louis and Columbia is any indication, the answer is a firm, monotonous "no."

I'm not the only person in the world, though. Let's look at a few other examples to see whether passive advertising works on other people. As with many things in my life, we'll begin by looking at the world of sports.

If you've watched a college or professional basketball game within the past decade, you know that broadcasters have managed to squeeze sponsored elements into every nook and cranny of the experience. Behind the scenes, brands dish out big bucks for screen time during games.

When a television network shows a star player's stats, some brand's logo typically accompanies the graphic. Replays after big moments and questionable calls sport yet another logo. As time runs out, another brand sponsors the "play of the game" highlight.

Just when you think it's over, the MVP of the game comes over for an on-camera interview — and the postgame report has its own sponsor. When your favorite team narrowly won the biggest game of your life, did you run out to buy toilet paper because Charmin sponsored an interview? Not likely.

Maybe you're not into sports. Perhaps you enjoy watching the local news every evening. If you think you're safe from flat ads in the form of commercials, think again.

Watch closely during the next weather report or traffic segment. Does the weatherman deliver his report on a logo-free screen, or did some local brand shell out a few thousand dollars to be featured during the broadcast? Based on my observations, most weather reports are sponsored.

Do TV viewers actually notice these subtle ads? If they do, are they engaged? Do they remember them 10 minutes after they turn off the TV? Can they name any of the brands they saw when they wake up the next morning? Probably not.

People watch the weather because they want to know the forecast. No one cares that a local flooring company spent money to be mentioned during a traffic update. No one feels a strong connection to the car company that spent millions of dollars[33] on advertising during the NFL playoffs. They do care about the traffic and the football games, but anything mentioned in the same breath as those aspects is just background noise.

This holds true even with captive audiences. We've talked about "going where the ducks are," so it naturally makes more sense to buy an advertisement in the stadium during a game, right? Fans are there for several hours at a time, and their eyes need to go somewhere when the action stops on the field or court.

Short answer: Nope. In-person flat ads don't engage viewers any more than they do on TV.

The long answer goes back to what we covered in the first few chapters. These ads, whether live or on TV, are missing one key ingredient: open minds. People watching basketball games aren't open to thinking about cars, software, insurance, law firms, genealogical societies, or witch doctors. Irrelevant brand reminders fade into the background in the presence of slam dunks or home runs. When fans return home, they talk about exciting plays and controversial penalties — not which soda company paid to have its logo next to the Jumbotron.

Brands that pour money into these advertisements fail to realize that life doesn't have to be this way. Passive sponsorships can transform into active sponsorships with a little extra effort. Rather than continue things as they always have been done, brands can choose the bolder option: engage consumers, capture audience attention, and transform the brand experience into the star of the show.

Evolving from Passive to Active

Without question, savvy experiential marketing campaigns bring flat sponsorships into the 3D world. Experiences empower brands to cut through the passive clutter and position themselves as memorable, worthwhile parts of other life experiences.

Let's pretend for a minute that you've just been hired as the CMO of Dr Pepper Snapple Group. Which of the following two options sounds like a better use of your marketing budget?

Option 1: Spend boatloads of money every year to put the Dr Pepper logo behind the end zone in multiple college football stadiums. On the plus side, plenty of people will see your logos. On the downside, no one will care.

Option 2: Spend less money to sponsor field goal competitions at halftime. Two randomly selected participants from the student section run onto the field sporting Dr Pepper jerseys — if one of them makes a successful field goal, he or she receives a giant check for $5,000. A few of these events take place in stadiums across the country, and they cause all eyes in the stadium to focus on the two aspiring kickers — and the brand.

By now, this hypothetical question should be a no-brainer. Without fail, those 60 seconds of amateur field goals capture the attention of the entire stadium. Everyone wants to see which ordinary person manages to sneak a kick through the uprights and take home the money. The audience gasps when someone barely misses and chuckles when a competitor shanks three kicks in a row. Even people who have no interest in sports cannot help but get excited (and a little jealous) when someone walks away with an extra $5,000 in his pocket.

Participants in these events might not drink Dr Pepper on the field, but they don't have to. The brand cured the halftime blues with quality entertainment. People who don't even like football put down their phones for a minute to watch two college students battle it out for enough money to buy a boatload of ramen noodles. Whenever fans in the audience recall this event, they'll remember the kids on the field wearing Dr Pepper jerseys and holding a check adorned with the Dr Pepper logo.

Experiences like these provide far more engagement than any static logo behind the end zone ever could. The TV audience might miss most of it, but the staying power of the experience for live attendees more than makes up for the difference.

Remember back in Chapter 1 when we talked about a fictional yogurt brand finding success at a local park? Parents received healthy samples while their kids played, and they later remembered the brand because they were open to the experience. I'm a huge advocate of getting out into the world and meeting target audiences face to face, but in-person interactions aren't always possible. People who watch the evening news are certainly open to unique experiences — but those experiences must match the environment.

In my case, the environment was a weather segment during a raging storm. Missouri is right in the middle of tornado alley, and we endure a few scary evenings every spring. High winds and hail damage countless homes, and you never know whether your area will be next.

During these storms, local channels frequently interrupt their regularly scheduled programming to bring viewers important updates. This around-the-clock weather coverage might be annoying to some, but people in the path of the storm remain glued to their televisions for up-to-the-minute coverage. This is how John Beal Roofing made its mark on me.

As hail battered my home last year, I turned to the weather report to see just how badly we would be pummeled that night. The news anchor said the hail would continue to fall for the next few hours. Throughout the broadcast, a banner ad for John Bean Roofing kept scrolling across the bottom of the screen.

Now, I'm not a fan of hail damage. I am, however, a fan of brilliant marketing. John Beal's advertisement could not have hoped for a more engaged audience in that precise moment. People were invested in the broadcast, and many of them had an immediate need for his services. The longer they watched the weather report, the more times they saw John Beal's name, phone number, and slogan. It was perfect.

After noticing the clever advertisement, I began to understand the strategy behind the positioning of this advertisement. The company knew that their logo next to the traffic cam might popup 10 times a day but probably would lead to zero new sales. Instead of wasting their money, they found a better, more relevant approach that puts their company front and center when their customers need them the most – during a storm. What's the difference? Their logo is not sneaking onto the screen out of context, hoping to trick viewers into remembering their brand the next time they need roof work. John Beal unapologetically inserts his brand into an outgoing narrative, engaging consumers by offering a helping hand during a time of need.

Just like the yogurt ambassador in the park, John Beal isn't selling to you — he's on your team. He wants you to rebuild your house after the storm, and his presence on the local news suggests that John Beal Roofing is the right company for the job.

Root, Root, Root for the Home Team

Speaking of local news and hometown pride, shared affiliations are invaluable assets to marketers who want to engage prospects.

Have you ever completely changed your opinion of someone after learning that you have the same favorite band or sports team? Maybe you both like to crochet. Perhaps you could talk for hours about your stamp collections. It's amazing what a little common ground can do for a relationship.

Psychological studies confirm[34] that shared interests lead to stronger emotional bonds. When two people connect over their hobbies, rooting interests, religious beliefs, or senses of humor, they become far more comfortable with each other. For individuals, that's a great way to meet new friends. For brands, it's a shortcut to audience trust and engagement.

Several brands in St. Louis have realized the advantages of rooting along as we watch our beloved Cardinals. To see this power in action, let's look back the team's acquisition of a slugger named Mark McGwire back in 1997.

As the 1998 season rolled along, McGwire and Sammy Sosa of the archrival Chicago Cubs became embroiled in a home-run race that remains one of the greatest sports storylines of all time. Sosa and McGwire both smashed Roger Maris' record as they dueled to see who would end the season with the most homers. Both men eventually were caught up in the great steroid scandal of the '90s, but all eyes of the nation were on McGwire and Sosa for a few seasons.

Cardinals fans became enamored with McGwire quickly during his tenure in St. Louis, and the man fondly known as "Big Mac" quickly became a folk hero. Kids and adults alike idolized McGwire for delivering high-powered offense every week. When he beat Sosa in home runs that year — 70 to 66 — locals loved him even more.

McDonald's capitalized on this obvious opportunity in grand fashion. While Sosa and McGwire duked it out for the home run record in 1998, the fast-food chain sponsored an entire section of Busch Stadium in McGwire's honor and renamed it "Big Mac Land." The section still exists today, underscoring two core ingredients of experiential marketing: the power of adding active elements to passive sponsorships and the potential of finding common ground with a target audience.

Many fans in 2018 weren't even alive when McGwire and Sosa competed 20 years before, but Big Mac Land remains a hit with Cardinals fans. Unlike baseball players, burgers never retire. Every time a Cardinals player knocks a home run into Big Mac Land, fans attending the game can redeem their tickets at McDonald's locations for a Big Mac. Millions of fans[35] have enjoyed free burgers over the years. And even though everyone in the stadium wins a free Big Mac, seats in Big Mac Land still fetch high prices — and every seat in the area includes a McDonald's gift package.

For Cardinals fans, Big Mac Land is where the fun happens. Props and souvenirs add an extra layer to the game experience. The passive sponsorship of the signage and branding in the area combine with the active experience of baseball and free swag to transform an otherwise ordinary section into a stadium landmark. Even people who don't buy tickets in the special section might say, "I had a great time! I sat a few seats away from Big Mac Land!"

McDonald's has created an experience that not only reaches people sitting in the section but also resonates with every fan in the stadium and anyone watching on television. The brand associates itself with fun, and McDonald's gains a bit more brand exposure every time someone says, "Big Mac."

Companies don't have to be as prominent as McDonald's to cultivate this level of fandom. Plenty of lesser-known brands cheer with fans at every home game and provide tangible rewards when their teams succeed. Convenience store chain On the Run, for instance, has been executing a popular promotion for years.[36] The deal, called "Six is a Serious Number," offers heavy discounts on soft drinks and coffees at participating stores if the Cardinals score more than six runs in a game.

When the Cardinals have five runs on the board and a player standing on third base, a palpable buzz fills the air at Busch Stadium. Regardless of their beverage preferences, fans know what that sixth run means — and they know the brand behind the promotion. They want the Cardinals to succeed, and they know On the Run is cheering right alongside them. That shared love of baseball brings brands and consumers together in a way no other marketing technique can.

St. Louis isn't the only town in America that loves its sports teams, of course. Los Angeles residents love the Lakers like no other, and few Lakers have been as important to California residents as Kobe Bryant. You might be surprised, then, to realize that Bryant occasionally found himself upstaged by Jack in the Box on his home court — at least temporarily.

Not every brand can inspire an entire basketball arena to chant about its products. Jack in the Box found a way to do just that by sponsoring a brilliant promotion at Lakers home games. If the Lakers hold their opponent under a certain score, every fan in attendance receives a bit of branded swag: a coupon for two free tacos from the fast-food chain.

Since Jack in the Box launched this promotion, it's not unusual to hear enthusiastic chants of "We want tacos!" echo throughout the arena during Lakers games.[37] Even in blowouts, fans stay until the bitter end because of the prospect of free tacos. If the opposing team is close to the score cutoff, fans cheer harder for the Lakers to make the defensive stops necessary to keep the opponent below the threshold.

Tacos from Jack in the Box might be the cheapest thing on the menu at $0.99 a pair, but nobody cares about the value of the prize — it's all about the experience. In those waning minutes of the games, Jack in the Box becomes an honorary Lakers fan and often upstages the team as the crowd shifts its support from the players on the court to tacos. If the opponent manages to break through the point threshold, boos rain down from the stands — but the positive feelings toward Jack in the Box persist.

Consumers are happy to team up with sponsoring companies, but those brands must provide a compelling reason to join forces. When brands go beyond passive sponsorships to actively align themselves with the hobbies, interests, and passions of their target audiences, they achieve deeper levels of engagement that would be impossible otherwise.

Efficacy Through Engagement

These stories all demonstrate the power of active engagement over passive consumption. As marketing budgets continue to tighten, I don't blame brands for gravitating toward seemingly "safe" options. After all, no one gets in trouble for purchasing space on a highway billboard, placing an ad in the local newspaper, or sponsoring the local weather report. Those investments are known commodities. They might not deliver great results, but no one questions why they happen.

Perhaps that's the problem, though. Marketers shouldn't be satisfied with "good enough." The status quo doesn't cut it anymore, and savvy brands of all sizes — from fast-food giants to local roofing companies — are thinking outside the box to inject more action in their sponsorships. A whopping 90 percent of professionals affirm that live events are critical to success, too.[38]

The question is, does *your* brand have the courage to ditch the ordinary and try something new?

CHAPTER 5

Extend the Moment

*"Users are much more likely to share posts with their
friends and engage in the comments if they connect to the story you're telling on a personal level."*
—*Joseph Ayoub, founder and CEO, Creaze*

When I founded my agency in 1995, I didn't have clients lined up
from day one. It took six months of pitches and conversations
before we finally landed a contract, but that first major victory ended
up being a dream client: Anheuser-Busch.

Over the 14 years that my agency worked with Anheuser-Busch, we
executed many campaigns that live on in my memory. One particular
incident rises above all the others, though. It was when I learned a life
lesson I'll never forget.

In 1998, Anheuser-Busch inked a sponsorship deal with Dale Earnhardt Jr., a NASCAR driver who hadn't yet stepped out of his legendary
father's shadow. Anheuser-Busch saw his rising stardom and decided
to make Earnhardt Jr. the face of the brand in the NASCAR arena.
Anheuser-Busch poured a ton of money into his car, covering it in that
unmistakable shade of Budweiser red and decking it out with brand logos

and emblems. It was a promotional work of art — a car that would have been at home in any marketing museum.

When the camera feed from the Goodyear Blimp showed the race, nobody could miss the Budweiser car flying around the track. To look at the car, you'd think we already had accomplished the marketing mission that we hoped to achieve. Well, you'd be wrong.

A few races into the season, I remember watching with pride as the green flag waved and the Bud-branded car zoomed around the track. Dale Jr. was building a solid fan base, and Anheuser-Busch was the driving brand behind his success. Everyone who loved Dale Jr. had a built-in affinity for Budweiser.

And then his car caught on fire. Three laps into one race — and still quite early in the NASCAR season — Dale Jr. crashed hard and totaled the car. He was fortunate to walk away from the crash unharmed, but the beautiful marketing masterpiece was destroyed. I assumed Anheuser-Busch's brand exposure died along with it; I was wrong.

In my mind, every race was guaranteed to provide at least three hours of exposure for Budweiser. I knew that cars sometimes crashed on the track, but I never expected it to happen to us. Three hours turned out to be more like three minutes, punctuated by several sad replays and slow-motion shots of Budweiser logos taking a beating before crews towed the car away. It wasn't exactly the brand exposure we had in mind.

The Anheuser-Busch marketing team was familiar with the NASCAR scene, though. They had seen plenty of crashes before, and they knew the higher-ups would be assessing the ROI of this sponsorship. While the leadership team likely expected to see hours of Dale Jr. racing in his terrific Bud-mobile, it wasn't a reality this time around. Thankfully, the marketing team had prepared for all contingencies.

Anheuser-Busch's marketing department designed a sophisticated formula to calculate ROI based on how many seconds — not minutes or hours — of airtime the car received in each race. When they reported back to the C-suite, they didn't say, "Dale Jr. crashed three minutes into the race. It was a complete waste of our budget." Instead, they compared the seconds of coverage to previous races and cross-referenced that coverage with the amount of money spent. It wasn't the ideal ROI, but it certainly was better than nothing. The executives might grumble a bit, but they would see the crash as a minor disappointment rather than a total failure.

In addition, my agency took strides to extend this sponsorship with a program that included point-of-sale opportunities in bars through beer specials. By creating the "Budweiser Pit Crew Challenge," visitors secured long-term memories with the brand. Participants competed with each other by jumping over a pit wall and replacing a tire on a Budweiser show car. A leaderboard showcased the fastest times while consumers took pictures with the show car, building brand affinity every step of the way.

Anheuser-Busch found success by looking at this sponsorship as a whole — beyond the anticipated airtime of a single race. Its fully integrated program included advertisements, driver appearances, bar promotions, grocery store deals, and VIP events that helped extend the sponsorship's experience in diverse ways.

What's the moral of this story? First, smart marketers find creative ways to report ROI to the people at the top — even if that means using metrics as hair-splitting as "milliseconds of exposure." In the end, something is always better than nothing.

More relevant to this book, however, is the lesson I took away from the event: When capitalizing on short-term sponsorship opportunities, the passive placement of a logo on an object (whether it's a sign, a T-shirt, or a race car) leaves too much to chance. Race cars crash, T-shirts get covered by jackets, and signs blow away in the wind. It's far more productive to take proactive measures to extend sponsorships beyond one-time events.

Don't leave the success of your marketing initiative to fate. Bring it to life by engaging your audience with a 360-degree focus and integration.

Multiple Eggs in Multiple Baskets

For an example of a one-time event that turned passive sponsorships into long-term engagement, let's turn to the world of boxing.

It was the fight of the century. A clash between two of the most talented, decorated, polarizing, and wealthy competitors in the world of combat sports: Floyd Mayweather and Conor McGregor.

Fight organizers and media outlets began building hype for the event long before either fighter committed to the match. Mayweather was the undefeated king of the boxing world, and McGregor seemed like the perfect challenger — a well-known MMA fighter with a chip on his shoulder the size of a boulder who was prepared to debut in the boxing ring against one of the greatest of all time.

When the two sides agreed to fight in Las Vegas on Aug. 26, 2017, everyone celebrated. Boxing and MMA fans came together, gamblers began making bets, and the marketing world wondered who would dish out the dough to sponsor one of the most-watched live events in television history.

When the smoke cleared, Corona won the rights of primary sponsorship. This brave brand committed to spending a cool $10 million[39] on the fight. That might seem like a big win for Corona, but would the brand see the ROI it wanted from a one-time event like a boxing match?

During all the hubbub, I stood on the sidelines as memories of my experience with Dale Jr.'s car came flooding back. Boxing matches are as unpredictable as NASCAR races (if not more so). What if Corona spent $10 million dollars only for Mayweather to land a knockout blow in the first round? Think of all that expense only to put Corona logos in front of 50 million[40] disappointed viewers for 30 seconds. Corona's marketing team would have a hard time justifying that one to the C-suite no matter how many "milliseconds of exposure" the brand received.

Fortunately for Corona, the fight didn't end in the first round. Or the second round. Or even the third round. Mayweather beat McGregor by TKO in the 10th round and the fighters duked out every minute of intense action surrounded by Corona branding.

Corona's marketing team doesn't deserve credit for sponsoring a boxing match that happened to go into double-digit rounds — nobody could have predicted that. They do, however, deserve credit for hedging their bets in case the fight came to an abrupt halt and for building a promotionally integrated program.

The brand found success in bringing its sponsorship to life before, during, and *after* the main event. Corona didn't just plaster its logos around the ring. Instead, VIP parties sporting Corona branding became the most sought-after events in Las Vegas for the week leading up to the fight. During the weigh-in, Corona generated social media buzz and garnered attention from fans with its own ring girls — dubbed "Corona girls." The beer brand ensured these women got plenty of airtime while sporting Corona-branded attire. After the fight concluded, Corona hosted post-fight parties to welcome supporters of both fighters to toast the match and talk about whether these two would meet in the ring again.

Corona's sponsorship wasn't just a success — it was an inevitable success. If you walked into Las Vegas with no prior knowledge of the sweet science, you would be forgiven for thinking Corona invented boxing. Corona had activations in bars all over Vegas, basically anywhere the beer brand was sold. Though the brand technically sponsored a one-time event, Corona's savvy marketing team figured out a way to own the pre-fight hype and the post-fight revelry. Thanks to smart planning, Corona didn't need to depend on the fighters to give the audience a good show; the beer company won long before Mayweather and McGregor entered the ring.

Factors completely out of your control can quickly transform terrific marketing opportunities into wastes of money. Smart marketers — like the team at Corona — take proactive measures to extend their exposure beyond singular events. Even when the worst-case scenario unfolds and your race car crashes, some careful planning allows you to engage consumers and make the experience worthwhile.

Remember the success we had with our state fair activations for Tractor Supply Company? State fairs take place outside, and weather conditions are impossible to control. We've had years where rain poured down almost every single day of the fair, which kept most people home and drove the few attendees who showed up back indoors. Those days are disappointing, but we plan for these contingencies to ensure nothing is a total wash.

Rather than keep our brand ambassadors out in the rain — where their sad, wet faces wouldn't create many positive brand impressions — we stock them up with merchandise and have them stroll around the covered areas of the fair. They distribute coupon booklets and chat with the brave souls who refused to let a little precipitation stop them from having a good time. Those people might not get the full-blown Tractor Supply Company experience, but they still have positive brand interactions and leave with some keepsakes that hopefully drive them to retail locations when the weather clears up.

> *The weather can be difficult because most of our state fair activations are outside. But that's also what brings it to life. It's kind of a yin and yang.*
>
> *If the footprint is completely closed due to a thunderstorm, Pro Motion has helped us to come up with creative solutions. We could partner with the fair and stand at the ticket gates to greet people when they come in to let them know that we're there. Perhaps, we could walk around to some of the different animal livestock 4-H and FFA buildings and facilities on the property instead of just being tied to our booth.*
>
> *The biggest thing for us is that it is a partnership. Whether it's a difficult conversation or it's about a successful campaign, we can always pick up the phone and have a conversation with Pro Motion's team — that's important. It's why we have continued to be successful with them for so many years in a row.*
>
> *—Tractor Supply Company*

Other brands might see a rainy day at the fair as a total loss, but 20 percent of expected engagement is infinitely better than none. By preparing for every eventuality, we ensure that we deliver ROI regardless of the situation — even when the roller-coasters shut down.

Be There or Be Square

I feel like I might have given T-shirts a bad rap in the last section. After all, who doesn't love a free T-shirt?

I cannot tell you how many times I've left an event — be it a fundraiser, a 5K run, or my son's baseball games — with a free T-shirt in my hand. These shirts usually serve as a big "thank you" to the sponsors who made the event possible, and every company's logo is printed on the back.

Sometimes, a lot of companies buy a share of shirt space. Ever seen a 10-year-old kid walking around with a T-shirt for a youth soccer team? Those shirts often have so many logos that you would need a magnifying glass to read them all.

Many companies sponsor these teams as a gesture of goodwill, but they often expect more than a little T-shirt real estate when they sponsor B2B professional events. Despite this expectation, companies have no problem writing checks to get their logos on event swag like pens, notepads, and Post-it notes. These utilitarian premiums require minimal thought, and brands assume that a few event attendees will somehow discover which brands align with their business needs based on a few branded goodies.

Smart brands aim to find common ground with their target consumers. T-shirts do turn people into walking billboards, but they aren't truly connecting with your brand. If you want to extend a moment of engagement — whether you're in the B2C or B2B world — you must start by *creating* a memory.

Before you ask, the moment when a person receives a light-up pen or branded koozie doesn't count. Instead, you must stir up the emotions of your target audience to create a *memory* that becomes ingrained in these items. In truth, many consumers think brands don't share their values, with 29 percent of B2B customers[41] believing that brands are limited to only offering products and services. This assumption creates a huge barrier to capturing leads and solidifying relationships.

Your brand has probably put its logo on countless of items — and that's fine. But it's time to ask yourself a question: How many times has your company actually attended one of the events it sponsors?

The only way to create positive emotional connections and lasting memories at a one-time event is to *be there*. This might seem obvious, but you'd be surprised at how rare it actually is. If you don't attend the event, nobody will know you beyond your logo — and that won't tell attendees all that much. Audience members must discover who you are, what you do, and what you're all about before they will attach any sort of emotion to their free T-shirts. Brand experience doesn't fall by the wayside when you decide to show up and participate in such events: Fifty-four percent of B2B marketers and 53 percent of brand managers[42] said they captured greater lead generation and an uptick in sales by being actively present among their targeted audiences.

Attending these events allows you to speak directly to your target audience and to make inroads with new customers and businesses. When you get in front of people, you become the local expert who is full of interesting information and offering cool swag. And if you've kept up with content marketing — as you should — you can encourage attendees to sign up for your newsletter or visit your website.

These connections lead to contact information, allowing you to continue the conversation after the event. Attendees who stick around to chat might want to know more about certain topics or products, and you can point them to your company blog for more information.

I know plenty of marketers who consider event attendance too far outside their comfort zones to be worth the risk. It's unfortunate, but a significant chunk of B2B consumers fail to engage with brands because companies simply don't use the right channels to get their attention. Hiding behind a keyboard loses potential consumers, but face-to-face meetings can foster true connection, communication, awareness, and sales. Are these marketers who oppose the act of "being there" risk averse, though, or are they simply out of practice?

Sure, you could hire an agency like mine. We could build a fun experience and engage your audience at the end of your sponsored 5K run with fun exhibits and games. People would have a great time and leave with lasting memories. Or you could take a simple approach and still achieve audience engagement. All you need are a few enthusiastic employees with branded clothing, a folding table, and a box of swag or free samples. The employees can enjoy quality one-on-one conversations with event attendees, and your brand gets great exposure for a fraction of the price. For a few hours of overtime pay and a quick raid of the supply closet, you can turn a passive sponsorship into active engagement.

Of course, not every short-term sponsorship opportunity revolves around physical events with thousands of attendees. In the 21st century, people spend just as much time in the digital world as the physical one. Thankfully, brands also have a place there.

For instance, branded entertainment is rising in popularity. Companies understand that most consumers skip or ignore commercials, so they are shelling out big bucks to ingrain themselves into shows and movies. Think of it as product placement with a hint of influencer marketing. Audiences watch shows while the on-screen personalities use and praise a brand's products. When executed correctly, it shouldn't feel like advertising.

Some shows keep their options open by using green screen stand-ins in lieu of actual products.[43] Actors drink from green cans or carry around green shopping bags while filming, and brands later bid to get their products or logos on the screen. Other brands can secure that same spot when the initial contract ends, which creates a recurring revenue stream and allows brands to pick and choose where they advertise.

This approach could help brands create hype in niche markets ahead of new marketing campaigns. If Coca-Cola wanted to get ahead of Pepsi before the Super Bowl, for example, the company could pay a sports-themed sitcom like "The League" to superimpose its branding on soda cans, billboards, and other areas of the show. Technology like this will continue to have interesting applications for multichannel brand activations in the future.

If you happened to watch the James Bond movie "Skyfall," you might have noticed two instances when Heineken beer appears on the screen. Would you be surprised to learn that Heineken footed approximately one-third of the production budget for the film?[44] Those two on-screen beer appearances weren't Heineken's only exposure for its money, of course. The brand also appeared in several short films around the film's release.[45]

These appearances were a fun way to promote the beer brand, but they're still passive advertising. Heineken could have done way more than just create awareness.

One of our clients, ShurTech Duck Brand duct tape, wisely turned its passive sponsorship of "Project Runway" into something much more. The company didn't sponsor the entire 2013 season of the show — it decided to sponsor an episode focused on unconventional materials. In that episode, contestants made prom clothes out of Duck Brand duct tape, which the show made abundantly clear with verbal and visual mentions of the brand throughout the broadcast.

This sponsorship was a great opportunity, but Duck Brand didn't want it to end there. The company wanted to show the world that duct tape is more than a tool for plumbers and construction workers; it can be a great way to express your creativity. The "Project Runway" episode was a step in the right direction, but Duck Brand was eager to extend the sponsorship — moving from passive to active — with real-life consumers. This is where my company came in.

We threw out several fun ideas before settling on a master plan. After the episode aired, we launched a 10-day pop-up shop in Manhattan's garment district. We picked this spot because we (correctly) predicted that the district would have a high per capita rate of "Project Runway" viewers. With our target area in mind, we knew we could take Duck Brand where the ducks were, if you will.

Our pop-up shop didn't exist solely to sell thousands of rolls of duct tape to fashionistas, however; that would have been a poor use of the space. Instead, we wanted to display beautiful works of Duck Tape fashion for passersby to see, enjoy, and use as inspiration. Throughout the week, we planned to host special events and meet-and-greets to make the most of the exposure.

Duck Brand loved the idea. With its blessing, we staked out the perfect location — an empty retail space with a ton of windows on a busy corner. We put together the inside of the shop while we built hype outside (we were just down the street from the Parsons School of Design). We put up Duck Brand and "Project Runway" signs outside the building, and we positioned brand ambassadors outside to deliver our message to passersby.

At first, we stayed intentionally vague to keep people's curiosity levels high. Once the interior was nearly complete and the big launch day was around the corner, we opened the floodgates. We promoted our upcoming VIP night, media night, and the dates when designers from the show would be in attendance. We revealed the runway inside the shop and let people know when real-life models would show off the amazing pieces of duct tape fashion created on the show. By the time we finished, everyone in the garment district couldn't wait to see our creation.

The store stayed open for 10 days. During that time, thousands of people attended to engage with the brand, see the models, and take photos. Duck Brand products flew off the shelves. To call the event a success would undersell just how effective this brand activation became. Duck Brand didn't just sell almost $100,000 worth of duct tape; it sold thousands and thousands of dollars of its product to a target audience that would drive awareness in a whole new market.

The "Project Runway" pop-up venue was basically a concrete blank slate at first. It was pretty much nothing. What it became was a beautiful rainbow of Duck Tape as our brand was brought to life so beautifully.

We used the pop-up store as a catalyst. We did a private viewing VIP cocktail hour just before the opening, and it was also a way for us to do a luncheon with the media. We included the creators of the dresses at that luncheon, which took us to that next level. The event was awesome and helped reaffirm that everybody loves Duck Tape. It was a lot of work, but it was well worth it — and the rewards were long-lasting.

—Duck Tape

Plenty of photos and videos from the event made the rounds on social media[46], furthering Duck Brand's reach into the creative world. People posted images of jackets, pants, wallets, and even ornate dresses made entirely of Duck Brand duct tape. The event only lasted for 10 days, but Duck Brand's target audience felt the engagement for much longer.

Join Social Circles

Social media has the power to transform a one-time, location-specific sponsorship into an enduring global phenomenon. Every tweet, snap, post, or photo created by a person at an event has the potential to reach hundreds or even thousands of viewers. If those viewers share the same post to their networks, the results grow exponentially.

Remember in Chapter 2 when we discussed how people trust the recommendations of others more than they trust branded content? That holds true even when consumers don't know the people making the recommendations. We prefer the faces of other humans over images on flat screens. Go figure.

Thanks to this tendency, social media has the power to transform an already active engagement into a global experience. The secret? Brands running the experiences must make it easy for attendees to invite their social media followers to join the action.

Social media in experiential marketing starts long before the event. Brands must tease their upcoming releases online, building hype among loyalists while establishing a base expectation of what's to come. This is a cheap way to garner attention for an upcoming experience, but it becomes even more effective with a small investment. By leaning on popular niche influencers among your target audience, you can spread excitement for an event in both local and online circles — even among people who don't plan to attend.

Imagine Kanye West, Kendrick Lamar, and Beyoncé have announced they are teaming up to do a one-night-only show. Hype among music fans automatically would make this the most anticipated event of the year. Now imagine what would happen if the event would not be televised and would be subject to a social media blackout (to the point of bouncers searching attendees for smartphones before letting them in).

Fans around the world would cry out in protest because they would be unable to participate. They would beg these musicians for engagement, and the musicians would miss out on millions of impressions — all because they chose to shun social media.

If this is such a horrible idea for musicians who already enjoy massive exposure, imagine how terrible the same approach would be for a growing brand. In a sense, this is exactly what brands do. While most companies aren't stealing attendees' smartphones, they frequently make it difficult for people to share their experiences on social media — and the consequences can be detrimental.

Most event attendees don't feel compelled to share their experiences online[47] because sponsors don't give them a reason to do so. At the same time, experiences depend on social media to make an impact beyond their target audiences. This is where virality can be incredibly useful.

Think of it like going to a game show, such as "The Price Is Right." The audience already loves the action on stage and wants to cheer for the contestants, but they sometimes need a little push. Signs facing the audience light up to tell them when to applaud, when to stay quiet, and when to shout their suggestions.

Event attendees don't need directions that explicit, but they could use a bit of guidance to remember to share online. Set up signs and include social media symbols on branded materials to encourage people to share their pictures and talk about the experience with their followers. If you have a photo opportunity — like when attendees met models draped in duct tape at our "Project Runway" activation — advertise hashtags people can use to share their photos.

Sticking with the game show theme, don't treat all audiences the same. People who attend a "Jeopardy!" taping don't respond to the same cues that work on guests at "Wheel of Fortune." If your experience attracts high-profile professionals, focus on the social platforms they use, such as LinkedIn and Facebook. If you want to reach a younger audience, set up custom Snapchat filters and promote Instagram hashtags.

Don't limit yourself to a single social media channel. Most attendees won't have a presence on every platform — especially not an active account. Instead, promote a few social media options to start the conversation and to put the voices of attendees to work for your brand.

Take Charge of Your Transformation

Experiential marketing can be a double-edged sword. Personal, immediate connections make these brand activations more effective than any other tactic, but factors beyond your control can intervene when you depend on a moment to make a memory. Dale Jr. crashed his beautiful red car. Mayweather vs. McGregor could have ended in its opening minute.

84 percent of brands consider experiences and events to play a significant role in their integrated marketing campaigns[1], so smart brands don't leave success up to chance. Just like Corona did before the big fight—and just as we do at the state fair—create contingency plans to stay in control of your experiences. Don't settle for passive sponsorships, which allow other forces to decide how your brand is perceived. Take

passive interactions and make them active by going a step further: Show up to the event, talk with attendees in person, and think of creative strategies that extend beyond plastering your logo on a sign.

Your target consumers would love to promote and remember your event, but they can only do that if you give them an experience worth remembering — and empower them to spread the word.

CHAPTER 6

Steal the Show

"The best marketing doesn't feel like marketing."
—*Tom Fishburne, founder and CEO, Marketoonist*

I was surprised to find that many examples of what I call "steal the show" opportunities are alive and well in the world of sports. However, it's clear that sports sponsorships and events provide an arena for brands to outscore competitors.

For example, Adidas and soccer go together like peanut butter and jelly. The two are so closely intertwined across the globe that it's almost impossible to imagine one without the other. Take a look at some of the biggest names in the sport who have partnered with Adidas over the years: Lionel Messi, David Beckham, Paul Pogba, Alessandro Del Piero, and Zinedine Zidane are all Adidas athletes, and they are responsible for many of the most iconic soccer moments of the 21st century. Adidas also sponsors many of the biggest soccer clubs in the world, including Manchester United and Real Madrid, and several national teams, such as Argentina, Spain, and Germany.

Adidas also is the primary sponsor of FIFA, the international governing agency of the sport. For the low price of about $70 million every four years[48], Adidas retains exclusive rights to advertising and merchandise in the World Cup — oh, and the brand has been the designer of the official World Cup ball since 1970.[49]

For decades, soccer and Adidas have been joined at the hip. So, naturally, the 2014 World Cup in Brazil was supposed to be all about Adidas. Before the tournament began, Ernesto Bruce, director of soccer at Adidas, went on record[50] to say, "This is where we put our stake in the ground and prove our domination in the market."

As you might have guessed by now, things didn't turn out that way. Adidas became too passive in its position as the official sponsor of the World Cup. Fellow athletic heavy-hitter Nike smelled an opportunity and did the unthinkable: stole the show from Adidas on the biggest athletic stage in the world.

Nike didn't take on Adidas directly, though. If it had, Adidas would have sensed the threat and pumped more money into marketing efforts to protect its throne. Instead, Nike used an integrated guerrilla-style campaign that included traditional sponsorships, video content, social media, and experiential marketing. Nike accomplished this all without ever mentioning the words "World Cup" in its advertisements — because it didn't have to. Adidas took care of marketing the tournament itself, and Nike slipped through the door Adidas left open.

While Adidas sponsored an impressive nine national teams in the 2014 World Cup, Nike sponsored 10, including the United States and host nation Brazil. Adidas had Messi, one of the top two players in the world, but Nike snagged Cristiano Ronaldo, the other member of that elite club. Nike even targeted players on teams sponsored by Adidas for individual shoe deals. Those players would sport the same uniforms as the rest of their teams, but their shoes (which allow more room for personal expression) were all Nike.

Leading up to the World Cup, Nike launched an online video campaign called "Risk Everything."[51] The campaign featured several glossy, high-octane videos that showcased Nike's new stable of international superstars. Put together, the videos garnered nearly half a billion online views and 22 million engagements[52] — including likes, comments, and shares — before the tournament even began. Some of the videos also aired on television, ensuring that Nike was on everyone's mind when the World Cup kicked off.

Thanks to top-notch content and associations with popular players, Nike's #riskeverything hashtag saw more than 650,000 uses leading up to the World Cup. These factors combined to boost Nike's Facebook following by 13.7 million users in only two months.

But why did Nike push so hard? Marketing leaders at Nike saw that Adidas was doing little to bring its World Cup sponsorship to life across the globe. The soccer giant had grown complacent, and Nike knew the time was perfect to claim its share of the soccer world.

To increase local engagement, Nike created a worldwide four-on-four tournament that it dubbed "Winner Stays." The simplicity of the format resonated strongly with fans already anticipating the World Cup, and 120 amateur teams from all over the globe went head-to-head for a chance to play in the finals on the flight deck of the USS Intrepid.[53]

Adidas pushed its World Cup involvement with a few commercials and social media posts, but Nike did all that and much more. When the World Cup finished, Nike left no doubt which athletic brand was the *real* star of the show. Adidas plastered its name all over one of the biggest events on earth, assuming its passive association would allow the brand to "prove its domination in the market." That approach left customers wanting more — and Nike gave them the engagement they craved.

Fast forward a few years, and Adidas clearly learned its lesson. For the 2018 World Cup, Adidas sponsored more teams than Nike[54], and Adidas marketers were feeling the pressure to engage or get left behind. Even though Adidas shifted strategies, it was unable to win back the share of the soccer market that Nike gained in 2014.

Perhaps Nike felt a bit of the heat, too. In summer 2017, Nike accidentally got a taste of its own medicine when Ronaldo tweeted a picture of himself as a child for a Nike ad. This sort of influencer endorsement would be great under normal circumstances, but Nike was caught trying to cover the Adidas logo on Ronaldo's sweatshirt with a large Nike swoosh. The internet quickly found the original picture and outed Nike, providing free publicity for Adidas as the World Cup drew closer.[55]

As Adidas learned in 2014, passive sponsorships in no way guarantee market dominance. Why? They fail to engage an audience. Look around your industry: How many of your competitors leave their customers unengaged and open to disruption? They might spend plenty of money on commercials, social media ads, and billboards, but adding those logs to the fire does nothing to fan the flames. With the World Cup, Nike walked up to the fire Adidas built and poured gasoline on it, riding a wave of engagement to become the star of the show. Adidas proved that it was vulnerable rather than dominant, and Nike became a true threat to the king of soccer.

Not many companies have the marketing budget of Nike, though. Small businesses likely cannot sign Ronaldo to multimillion-dollar deals, create Hollywood-quality video campaigns, or sponsor 30 soccer tournaments in the world's largest cities. That's the beauty of using experiences to disrupt the competition, though. You don't need to outspend them — you just have to *outthink* them. By giving other companies' customers the experiences they are missing, you can swoop in and steal audience members from right under the competition's nose.

Turn Some Heads

No one remembers when everything goes according to plan. When we create a strategy and execute it perfectly, those experiences fade into the background. We remember the unusual far more easily than the mundane.

At some point in your life, you probably saw someone in an environment you never expected. As a child, it likely blew your mind to see a teacher shopping at the grocery store or walking in a neighborhood park: *"What do you mean, teachers don't live at school?!"* In your adult life, maybe you saw your buttoned-up manager thrashing in the mosh pit at a local metal show or a "mostly vegetarian" friend standing triumphant at a wing-eating competition. We remember these events so clearly because, though we recognize the people and the scenarios, we must work harder to see them in the same place at the same time.

The marketing equivalent to this phenomenon is simple: an in-person experience in an unexpected location. You still need to go to a place where minds will be open, as we discussed in Chapter 1, but you can pick a location that might cause people to pause and say, "Wow! Never thought I'd see you here!" This juxtaposition can add a new layer of excitement to an activation.

Any ideas spring to mind? Think about places where your customers are most likely to be open-minded about your product but surprised by your presence. Here's an obvious one: right in your biggest competitor's backyard.

Say, for instance, a Pepsi event in the heart of Atlanta. Since the late 1800s, Coca-Cola has been an Atlanta staple. The company owns a 29-story headquarters in the city, employs thousands of Atlanta locals, and maintains a 20-acre museum dedicated to all things Coke. Every local event or major street boasts some sort of Coca-Cola signage. Atlanta is almost as crazy about Coke as St. Louis is about the Cardinals — *almost*.

If you're the head of marketing at Pepsi, do you view the Atlanta market as a lost cause? Or is it an opportunity for your brand to stand out from the crowd? Peachtree TV (one of our clients) presented this exact opportunity to Pepsi — and Pepsi wisely seized the opportunity.

From 2008 to 2010, we orchestrated one of the most popular events in Atlanta: Peachtree TV's "Screen on the Green" outdoor movie series. For five weeks every summer, Peachtree TV screened free movies on a large screen in a public park. Up to 15,000 people attended each screening, with 50,000 attendees stopping by at some point during the summer. In other words, "Screen on the Green" was an ideal sponsorship opportunity for many brands aside from Peachtree TV.

The year Peachtree TV approached Pepsi, the event was held at Centennial Olympic Park — right next door to the World of Coca-Cola, the brand's famous museum. The park is so close[56] that you could easily hit the museum with a well-thrown soda can. We weren't just in Coca-Cola's backyard — we were in Coke's living room with our feet on the couch, eating food we took from the fridge.

Pepsi was eager to ride in like a Wild West outlaw in a hostile town. We put up a ton of signage, interacted with the local crowd, and handed out pallets upon pallets of free Pepsi products.

It probably goes without saying, but Coke was not thrilled with Pepsi's bold sponsorship. It couldn't stand the fact that 50,000 Atlantans were having a fun, memorable, and Pepsi-themed experience right next door.

Pepsi executives, on the other hand, could not have been happier. Several of the higher-ups flew in one week to witness a Pepsi party in Coca-Cola's hometown. Can you imagine a better dream scenario for a marketer? To have your C-suite high-fiving one another and celebrating your brilliance while your biggest competitor steams across the street?

One Pepsi executive said it best: "Being able to get our product in the hands of 15,000 people on any given Thursday night is more than you can imagine ... it's off the charts, is what I would say. Totally off the charts!" Sounds like a nice change of pace from constantly defending the marketing spend.

Furthermore, Pepsi didn't have to do anything unusual at the event. Our brand ambassadors mingled with the crowd, gave out samples and swag, and encouraged attendees to enjoy themselves. The only thing that made this experience different was the location, but it made all the difference in the world.

Similar opportunities exist in every industry. Imagine an ocean wildlife protection event held near Death Valley National Park or a southern BBQ joint handing out slices of brisket at a farmers market in Boston. Seek opportunities to make your audience ask, "What are you doing here?" Once you have their attention, deliver experiences they won't forget. By using location to your advantage, you can turn ordinary events into extraordinary experiences (and maybe irk the competition in the process).

Ride Someone Else's Wave

If you're not quite ready to antagonize your biggest competitors in their domain, you can still ride someone else's wave to garner attention in a less aggressive manner. You can also boost the effectiveness of your own experiences by using existing attractions as stepping stools.

Way back in 2008, the political world was on fire as Barack Obama and John McCain competed for the highest office in the U.S. As the presidential election drew nearer, the nation became increasingly divided. Even people who normally kept out of politics found themselves dragged into daily political debates. Would Obama really become the first black president? Could McCain keep the Republicans in the White House despite George W. Bush's waning popularity? Questions like these became part of everyday life in America that year, and CNN saw an opportunity to ride the wave.

As part of a two-year campaign, CNN partnered with our agency to activate an experiential program called "Election Express Yourself" during the midterms and the 2008 election. To deliver on the objective, we transformed an Airstream trailer into a mobile recording studio. We then traveled the country and invited people to record themselves voicing their political passions. Once we had captured the video, we sent digital files to CNN's headquarters to be edited and showcased during branded segments.

People loved expressing their opinions with a chance to get on TV, so we had limitless geographical options. Talk about going where the ducks were — we would have had trouble finding a place where the ducks *weren't*. We spent months crisscrossing the country, asking average Americans to talk about the economy, healthcare, foreign affairs, and anything else they viewed as important. By the time we finished, we had spoken to 50,000 people and traveled nearly 10,000 miles.

Our CNN campaign was a mobile tour at its finest, but its relevance to this section — the moment we rode someone else's wave — happened on election night.

On a normal day, Times Square in New York City is a total zoo. You could visit at 10 a.m. on a Tuesday and find excitement on every corner. We knew that election results would cause the place to go nuts like nowhere else in the country. We didn't just go to Times Square, though, we got a permit and parked our Airstream right in the middle of it.

Throughout the day, we had a ton of people visit the Airstream. We shot quick videos that hit the airwaves on CNN mere moments after we recorded them. People loved having a platform to express their opinions on the most relevant day of the year. This wasn't an attempt to disrupt a CNN competitor, like Fox or NBC; we wanted to find a spot abuzz with activity, so we planted our experience and let people come to us.

The moment Wolf Blitzer called the election for Barack Obama at about 11 p.m., the crowds poured into the already overflowing Times Square. We witnessed hugging, cheering, fighting, you name it — every expression of human emotion happened in the area.

For safety reasons, New York City gave us a 5,000-person limit in our CNN-branded area. All day long, we had done an admirable job of sticking to that rule. When the results came in, however, crowd control flew out the window. We had nearly 15,000 people crammed into our space, and police had to shut down traffic through the area because the event had grown so large. Yes, we shut down traffic in both directions at the wedge in Times Square.

In the middle of that chaos was the CNN experience, emblazoned with the CNN logo and carrying the voices of the people in Times Square. On that night, CNN culminated an already successful tour by placing itself at the center of the election universe. One of CNN's executives called Election Express Yourself the "crown jewel[57]" of the network's promotional strategy — high praise from the network that won the 2008 battle for best election coverage.

Partly thanks to the experience we provided, CNN beat every other network on election night that year. The network reached its highest primetime ratings in history, taking the 10 p.m. timeslot crown from Fox.

Just as Pepsi was the focal point in Atlanta, CNN became the focal point in New York — but for entirely different reasons. In one place, we stood out because we didn't belong. In the other, we stood out because our presence made perfect sense and offered exactly what people wanted: a chance to react to the election results.

The key to riding someone else's wave is not minimizing the competition's impressions — it's all about maximizing your own. Find an event that already draws a crowd of your target customers, and look for an opportunity to insert your brand into the fray. You will drive engagement in the moment, and your brand will be remembered as part of the larger picture. When building a brand, those associations can go a long way toward winning over new audiences.

Become the Talk of the Town

So far in this chapter, we've covered how to use in-person marketing events to upstage the competition in bold ways, how to ride the coattails of big events for branding advantages, and how to stand out by doing familiar things in unfamiliar environments. Most of the examples I've used so far have focused on major multinational brands. However, not every show needs to be stolen; some shows simply need a smart sponsor to come in and make an event its own.

If Atlanta is Coke country and St. Louis is Cardinals nation, then Avon, Ohio, is definitely Duck territory. No, I'm not talking about "going where the ducks are." Since 1996, Avon has served as the world headquarters for Duck Brand duct tape, our friends from the "Project Runway" example in Chapter 5.

For decades, the biggest annual event in Avon had nothing to do with Duck Brand. The Festival of Flowers, as it was called, drew a large regional crowd of people who came to Avon literally to smell the roses. Perhaps a few of them bought the same tulips from QVC that I did. We may never know.

As the years went by, the Festival of Flowers began to wither away. Greenhouses were demolished and replaced by regular houses, and flower aficionados came to Avon in smaller droves every season. By 2004, the festival had almost fizzled out completely — until Duck Brand decided to do something about it.

Town leaders were looking for sponsors to hold an event to replace the Festival of Flowers. They couldn't go back to the way things were — low turnouts at recent festivals proved that much — but Avon still had the infrastructure and desire to host an annual event. People just didn't know what that event would showcase.

Duck Brand knew it held a high position in the city's business community, so leaders at the company offered to revive the festival with one major change. The event would no longer focus on flowers — it would revolve around the product that made Duck Brand famous: duct tape. With an agreement in place, the city of Avon and Duck Brand gave birth to the Avon Heritage Duck Tape Festival.[58]

The event is completely free to attend, with about 50,000 visitors descending on Avon (a town normally home to about 20,000 people) on Father's Day weekend to revel in the glory of duct tape. Everything from art to fashion gets a makeover courtesy of duct tape. Live music entertains thousands of Duck Brand fanatics, while kids ride roller-coasters and enjoy fried treats.

> *I like to say that every year the festival gets better and better. I think back to the first one where the staff here at the company just had a small craft area where we were making bracelets for people visiting the festival.*
>
> *We now have a giant tent where hundreds of people can go in and just make their own creations and play with Duck Tape. Larger-than-life themed artwork is present throughout the fairgrounds, and it's all made from Duck Tape. To have an entire event focused around your products is so exciting, and the amount of time and energy our guests put into making costumes and artwork is humbling. It was clearly a learning experience for us, and now the event is pretty much a well-oiled machine.*
>
> *—Duck Tape*

I love visiting this event. The amount of time, energy, and creativity attendees pour into the festival astounds me. People show up wearing clothes made entirely of duct tape. Some are infants, and some are more than 80 years old. Just last year I met a man and woman in their 80s who attended the festival dressed from head to toe in duct tape. The man had a suit jacket, complete with a vest, while the woman sported a parasol — all made using Duck Brand duct tape. It's amazing how the local community has embraced the brand and how people travel from far and wide to take part in this celebration.

Duck Brand could not have sponsored a better opportunity. Not only is Duck Brand the talk of the town in its local market, but the company also transformed an existing event into a celebration of its own product.

Duck Brand might not have the same budget as Nike or Pepsi, but the company discovered a way to ride someone else's wave all the same. You don't need to spend mountains of money or start a brand war with another company to get noticed and engage with consumers — you need to surprise people in a positive way. Seek out opportunities to become the talk of the town, drive engagement, and create fun memories for attendees.

Finding the Right Opportunity

All is fair in love and war, and marketing is a bit of both.

If your competitor or industry leaves an opening for your brand to steal the show, you don't want to let someone else take advantage of the opportunity. Seize the day and enjoy watching the executive team high-five one another over your brilliant marketing strategy. Rest assured that nobody from Nike or Pepsi had to ask forgiveness for their bold moves. They executed smart strategies that engaged their audiences and created lasting memories. What more could anyone want?

As I mentioned before, you must pick your battles wisely when you step into enemy territory. You want the right opportunity rather than just *any* opportunity. You need a space where you don't have to compete for attention to ensure your experiences don't get lost among those of 20 other brands. If you pick your spot correctly, you won't have to worry about targeting the right people — you'll be in the middle of a crowd that's curious about what you have to say.

If you choose to ride someone else's wave, you can't sit idly by and expect everything to work itself out. How can you draw attention to your experience in this environment? With Pepsi, bold branding and a prime location were enough. Nike worked much harder to undermine Adidas at the World Cup. Our CNN experience drew curiosity by presence alone, but we earned their full attention when we gave people a voice.

When you identify the reason audiences should pay attention — that differentiating factor that makes your brand the star of someone else's show — you're ready to start building an emotional connection. The path from experience to brand familiarity to brand loyalty is clear. All you need to do is deliver the experience.

PART III
INSPIRE

CHAPTER 7

Lend a Helping Hand

"Socially conscious marketing is a powerful way for businesses to shape their brand and connect with consumers on a deeper level." —Steve Olenski, contributor, Forbes

Good intentions are wonderful, but brands should not support charitable causes solely because those partnerships might help them gain favor in the eyes of consumers. The more companies understand their obligations to make the world a better place, the happier everyone will be.

It is important to acknowledge that modern consumers expect more from brands than reasonable prices and reliable products. They want to do business with companies and people that care about the world. Helping others intrinsically is the right thing to do, but this is a book about marketing — so I would be remiss to gloss over the marketing benefits that accompany good deeds.

Social consciousness in business is more important today than in decades past because of the speed at which news travels. Information flows freely these days, and stories of suffering reach audiences across the world in seconds. Whenever a disaster strikes somewhere on earth, you can hop on Twitter to get live updates and open a second tab and see the latest news reports on the event. By the time the daily newspaper arrives in the morning, you already know whether the wildfire in Los Angeles was contained — you figured it out after dinner last night by following Los Angeles Times journalists on Twitter and watching streams on Facebook Live to see the rescue crews in action.

This fast-paced information stream can be a beautiful thing, but it's also a double-edged sword. The old newspaper saying of "If it bleeds, it leads" has never been truer.

News websites rely on our survival instincts to tell us about things that could threaten our lives. Anyone who uses the internet knows that negative headlines tend to dominate the news cycle. Why? According to a study that appeared in AdWeek[59], negative headlines get significantly more clicks than positive headlines. This incentivizes media outlets to rely on negative headlines to make more money from advertisers, creating an online impression that the world is scarier than reality.

Media outlets know that humans gravitate toward bad news, but that doesn't necessarily indicate an increasing number of disasters across America and throughout the rest of the world. Readers interpret the flood of bad news as a sign of a dangerous environment, which causes them to look for more scary headlines, which causes them to feel more concerned. This cycle heightens their survival instincts at the expense of their minds and bodies.

In 2014, a group of Canadian researchers found that frequent exposure to images of violent events leads to increased levels of anxiety, social dysfunction, depression, and weekly alcohol consumption.[60] Most importantly, this study found that frequency of exposure — not duration — was the key driver of the negative effects. In other words, someone who watched a long video about a single violent event would feel less anxious and depressed than someone who encountered multiple brief instances of violent content.

In the online world of Twitter and other social sites, users have almost limitless pools of distressing news to consume. When someone browses Twitter, Facebook, Reddit, or other social sites with news elements, he or she can simply load the page and start scrolling to see an endless stream of bad news with accompanying thumbnail images.

It's an all-you-can-eat buffet of negativity. Though users consume this content willingly, the research proves that brief exposure to a slew of negative headlines takes a toll. People who consume news this way suffer mentally and physically via elevated stress levels. Their well-being and outlooks on life worsen with every scroll.

Of course, stories of hardship and injustice are part of life. News outlets would be sleeping on the job if they failed to broadcast this content to the masses. Outlets and influencers focus on these stories because they know consumers will keep clicking on them, but the connection between ad revenue and fear is dangerous.

Perhaps you've noticed how the internet can go ablaze for 24 hours about a specific scandal, tragedy, or heartbreaking event and then forget all about it the next day. It's almost frightening how quickly our brains can move on from things we once considered to be critically important threats.

Consequentially, this onslaught of bad news has created a situation eerily similar to the one I described earlier in this book. Just as the exceedingly crowded digital marketing climate makes it difficult for brands to engage emotionally with consumers, this flood of negative news overwhelms our senses. Everything blends together until a series of bad events becomes an indistinguishable blur of tragedy and danger.

Eventually, even the most heinous crimes and injustices fail to stand out. This haze makes consumers feel even less engaged with what's happening in the world. They still click on headlines, but they don't remember what they read. That sort of superficial engagement is exactly what brands want to avoid.

Become the Beacon of Hope

When every news station, social media outlet, and town crier is spreading negativity, how can brands add something positive, memorable, and engaging to the equation?

In the past, companies have taken an important (yet passive) role in the salvation of the world: financial support. Companies are quick to write checks and send them to areas affected by disasters, or they create promotions and funnel a certain amount of their proceeds to organizations like the American Red Cross.

There is nothing wrong with this approach — it's actually necessary. Any donation to a reputable organization is a positive step, and the charities doing work on the front lines can always use more money to maximize their efforts. This book is still about marketing, though. While big checks and heartfelt condolences are meaningful, they do not provide much marketing value to the companies making the donations.

These passive disaster relief efforts simply aren't memorable. A few articles might crop up about a generous donation from your business, but not much press attention follows. Most of the time, those articles are less about the companies donating than about the disaster itself — lumping in one company's donation alongside a list of others.

As commendable as that donation might be, it's neither surprising nor engaging when a brand writes a check. Consumers expect big companies to show their support in times of need: "Of course that company donated $100,000 to disaster relief: It's worth $3 billion! That's not a big deal." Some charitable donations can even backfire if consumers feel like a brand does not donate an amount proportionate to its size.

When a brand takes the passive route of writing a check, the resulting media coverage is just another dull story on a consumer's fast-moving windshield. Unlike the bugs of bad news that splatter and stick in their minds, charitable donations are like grains of sand — they bounce off the glass, unnoticed and forgotten.

As we have covered in detail, the only way to stick to that windshield and capture consumer attention for more than a few seconds is to bring outreach efforts to life by donating time and physical effort. Consumers know (or at least believe) that most companies have an abundance of money. When a company demonstrates a willingness to commit its time as well as its dollars, however, people pay attention.

One of my favorite examples of charitable brand outreach done right is Tide's Loads of Hope program.[61] When Hurricane Katrina struck New Orleans, many families were forced to spend days wearing the same unwashed clothes. They were so busy securing food, water, and shelter that they didn't have time to wash anything — much less have a dependable place to do so.

In response, Tide created a mobile laundromat and sent it into the region to help victims of the disaster regain a sense of normalcy. A truck equipped with 32 washers and dryers cleaned more than 300 loads of laundry a day, working with Federal Emergency Management Agency to optimize its placement in areas that could help the most people.

After its success in Katrina relief, Tide added a second truck and kept the program going. Loads of Hope has helped victims of tornadoes, floods, hurricanes, and other disasters. The Tide brand continues to reap the benefits of being a donor and an active participant in rebuilding affected areas.

Tide can send its trucks anywhere in the U.S. at a moment's notice, but the company also has found ways to lend a hand when disaster strikes overseas. After the massive earthquake hit Haiti in 2010[62], Tide discovered that staff members at a 700-bed hospital were hand-washing bed sheets and linens because their laundry equipment had been destroyed. Within a few days, Loads of Hope shipped several industrial-sized washing machines to the hospital, allowing workers to spend less time dealing with dirty linens and more time caring for victims.

Loads of Hope has enjoyed plenty of positive media coverage over the years, positioning Tide as a brand that truly cares about consumers. The most attention-grabbing part of the Loads of Hope campaign isn't the media coverage, though: it's the tens of thousands of families who have been touched by the program. The value of the emotional connections the brand created with those consumers is immeasurable and completely genuine.

Let's put ourselves in the shoes of a person helped by Loads of Hope. I've never been affected by a flood or similar natural disaster, so I can only imagine what it feels like to have every article of clothing you own covered in mud and water. And not only your clothes, but also your children's clothes. You don't have running water to drink or shower — much less to wash your shirt. You're stuck with the dirty clothes on your back, a constant reminder of the upheaval in your life.

It's easy to see how Tide's mobile laundromat would be a godsend. I might have used a different detergent in the past, but I'm going to be a

Tide loyalist for life if they help me wash my family's clothes in the wake of a tragedy. I would never forget the time when Tide allowed my family a small relief during an otherwise terrible situation.

After I heard about Loads of Hope during Katrina, I called a contact with a major battery brand and pitched the idea of building a power truck to grant disaster victims access to electricity, batteries, and free Wi-Fi during massive outages. That company didn't bite, but one of its competitors saw the value: Since 2011, Duracell's PowerForward[63] program has distributed more than 450,000 batteries to about 34,000 families in the U.S. and Puerto Rico.

These programs might only garner modest media coverage, but that's not the point of this goodwill gesture. If there is a business benefit from these outreach efforts, it's the increased loyalty from the people who receive the aid and have formed emotional connections with the associated brands. Those individuals might even become brand advocates, spreading the word about how much those companies care.

Whether people talk about a brand or never mention it, helping those in need is the right thing to do. Companies that treat disaster relief efforts as photo ops never get far — and can actually do more damage to their brands than if they had taken no action. Only brands that help for the sake of helping stand to gain anything from their involvement.

Why Authenticity Matters

Today's consumers have highly sensitive BS detectors. Audiences are long past the point of believing that they're the 1 millionth customer, and they are quick to call out brands that appear too self-serving or out of touch with reality.

Remember when Sean Penn flew to New Orleans with an entourage (including a personal photographer) to help rescue Katrina victims? People interpreted the gesture as insincere, and the internet roasted the actor for attempting to use the disaster to bring attention to himself.

In all fairness, I don't know Sean Penn. He might have genuinely wanted to help people affected by Katrina. It's also possible that his entourage is always with him and that he thought nothing of bringing them along for the ride. Unfortunately, showing up with a big group of people and a cameraman rubbed some folks the wrong way.

The tabloids slammed Penn for his antics, and some Katrina victims even mocked him[64] as he floated around the city with his crew. Bystanders called out to Penn and his crew in their boat, asking how they planned to fit any survivors in a craft already packed with people. Penn eventually offered a strongly worded defense of his trip[65], but it was too late at that point. People already had formed their opinions, and no amount of explanation would change their minds.

Experiences like Sean Penn's explain why many brands are content to simply write a check and keep their involvement in relief efforts to a minimum. They don't want to put themselves in harm's way. What if a journalist views the outreach as self-serving? What if someone captures a photo of relief workers goofing off? Even if the efforts to help are sincere, these possibilities pose great risks to the brands behind them.

Many companies avoid disaster relief because they fear they will come across as inauthentic and commercially driven. Their fears might be founded in reality, but the solution is simple: It all comes down to authenticity. If a brand does something to get publicity, people will interpret the outreach that way. If a brand does something to help and avoids the spotlight, news of the good deeds will spread on its own.

If your brand heads into a disaster zone, leave the camera crews at home. The photos that emerge from an outreach effort should come from people living in the moment instead of someone on your payroll.

More importantly, don't dispatch an army of representatives in branded clothing to hand out supplies, make a quick speech, and then rush back to the warmth and safety of your office. If you reach out, do it all the way. Devote several days to the efforts, staying long after the cameras are gone. You aren't a premier brand at a charity auction — you are just another group of volunteers making a difference.

Schedules and plans can reek of inauthenticity. You cannot attempt to maximize exposure in multiple areas — camera crew or not — and expect people to interpret superficial help as a genuine investment in their recovery. Consumers see right through commercialized plans. To reap the marketing benefits of disaster assistance, you must abandon all desire for those benefits.

When deciding whether to take an active or passive involvement in a disaster, ask yourself one question: Is there an authentic connection between your brand and this tragic event?

The connection could be as simple as geography. No one blasted Tim McGraw for being outspoken[66] and physically present during Katrina. Why? He's from Louisiana. The people affected were *his people*, so he naturally wanted to help. Likewise, no one called J.J. Watt's $37 million fundraiser for Hurricane Harvey relief[67] a publicity stunt — he has called Houston home for his entire NFL career. The NFL even named Watt as its "Man of the Year" for his efforts[68], and fans around the league applauded him for using his influence to help others. And when St. Louis Cardinals catcher Yadier Molina got involved in Puerto Rico relief efforts[69], it didn't feel like a PR stunt because Molina is from Puerto Rico. All three men genuinely cared about their communities, had an emotional connection to them, and provided hands-on involvement during times of need.

Without an apparent geographic connection, brands must get more creative. Tide and Duracell provide great examples of how to do this: Neither company had direct ties to the regions where they began their relief efforts, but both provided services that made sense in the context of their industries. These brands show how to be an authentic beacon of hope during tough times. We will cover more ways to make non geographic connections later in this book.

The ROI of Doing Good for the Right Reasons

If your brand wants to lend a helping hand when disaster strikes, it might be difficult to nail down the initial ROI of these efforts. Articles, photos, and tweets are solid byproducts of your work (though they should never be your goal), and they *can* help show the ROI behind your good deeds. Remember what I said in Chapter 2 about how people trust their friends more than they trust brands? Let the publicity occur organically. This will ensure that people see your outreach as genuine and praiseworthy.

Brands are still businesses, though, and businesses cannot completely ignore ROI. Fortunately, even the most charitable actions provide measurable perks to the benefactors. Disaster relief ROI typically falls into two main categories: the numbers you share with the world and the numbers that help you keep your job (or show off your marketing prowess).

Public metrics should focus on the non-branded results people care about. Consumers are likely curious about how many people benefitted from your presence in a disaster area, for instance. Tide happily tells the world about how many loads of laundry people have done in its mobile laundromats, and Duracell tracks the number of batteries it has handed out to people in need. These results look good for the brands, and their successes might encourage others to follow in their footsteps.

Internally, brands should keep track of sales trends in the areas they've visited and social media mentions of their presence. Whoever tracks those numbers should deliver them to company leaders inside confidential memos that say, "For internal use only." Executives who make top-level decisions have a fiduciary responsibility to their stockholders, and they generally want more than good vibes at the end of an outreach program. They want something that shows shareholders that their humanitarian efforts did not come at the expense of the company's success.

To keep outreach efforts alive and helpful, marketers must learn to deliver financial data to higher-ups that justifies the involvement of their brands. The C-suite won't be satisfied with the number of hugs and thank-you's your team received — they want information that supports future involvement.

Always remember: What gets measured gets funded. Do good for the right reasons, but find ways to track the results carefully to ensure you can show company leaders that a socially responsible brand is a successful one.

After reading this section, you might feel compelled to jump at the next opportunity to wedge your brand into disaster relief. You also might fear the risks and decide to stick to passive involvement in every circumstance. Don't choose one path or the other ahead of time; evaluate each opportunity to help based on whether your company's assistance would be authentic, welcome, and useful. Once you've committed to a cause, measure the results of your involvement to determine whether the outreach qualified as a branding success.

CHAPTER 8

Align With a Cause

"Corporate social responsibility is a hard-edged business decision. Not because it is nice to do or because people are forcing us to do it ... but because it is good for our business. —Niall FitzGerald, former CEO, Unilever

You know who gets more hate than they deserve? Millennials. I feel bad for the younger generation. Whenever an industry fails or an American cultural pastime fades away, older people lay the blame at the feet of Millennials. Department stores are going out of business[70] because people prefer to shop online? It's those damned Millennials and their smartphones! Movie theaters are shutting down[71] because Netflix is cheaper and more convenient? Millennials don't understand the value of the theater experience!

If you listen to Baby Boomers, Millennials are even killing marriage[72] and the American tradition of an honest 9-to-5 workday.[73] From entertainment staples to shopping options to social norms, anything that doesn't look like it did in the '80s is likely because of Millennials.

Who knew our children would grow up to be such monsters?

In all seriousness, Millennials are in the driver's seat of society right now — and they mean business. The Millennial generation is the largest in U.S. history[74], and this group is just now reaching its prime spending years. The modern marketplace is full of Millennials with money to burn. If companies don't listen to Millennial demands and adapt to their habits, those businesses will miss out on the largest available piece of the consumer pie.

Millennials care deeply about convenience, technology, and a special shade of pink.[75] They care even more about the environment and social justice — and they expect brands to share those concerns. Ninety-one percent of Millennials gravitate toward brands that support a cause[76], and most would happily spend more money to buy from a socially conscious company. This generation backs up its convictions with its cash, so brands must stand for something if they want to attract Millennial buyers.

Those convictions aren't limited to consumerism, either. Millennials also represent the largest generation in the U.S. workforce.[77] Your best young salespeople, designers, coders, and managers feel strongly about social causes at work and at home. The people you are grooming to lead your company in the future expect the organization to care about the same things they do — or they'll find a new employer who shares those values.

According to the 2016 Cone Communications Millennial Employee Engagement Study[78], 64 percent of Millennials consider a company's environmental policies before taking a job. In addition, 83 percent would be more loyal to a company if it helped them contribute to the social issues important to them. The best Millennial employees will lead the most successful companies of the future, which means brands that appeal to Millennial preferences now will be in good shape when the next generation reaches the C-suite.

What's the best way to reach this generation of caring people? As we covered in the last chapter, today's information-rich digital arena allows news to travel at the speed of light. Bad news gets the most clicks, but brands don't want that kind of exposure. To gain the attention of these young workers, brands must join the growing number of companies making headlines for corporate social responsibility (CSR).

CSR is not a new concept. Back in the 1950s, CSR missions became more prevalent[79] when the public and the government began to scrutinize the activities of corporations closely. Things really took off in the 1980s, when a program called Superfund[80] arose to hold companies accountable for their environmental impact. Thanks to the Environmental Protection Agency and Superfund, several companies were forced to pay financial reparations for violations of environmental law and to develop newer, safer practices.

Modern CSR is stronger than ever. Between the rise of the digital era and the Millennials who grew up amid this change, brands cannot ignore the wide-reaching benefits of joining the cause. Companies that demonstrate their respect for social and environmental causes — the same causes near and dear to the hearts of Millennials — have the power to transform loyal customers into brand fanatics.

Embracing CSR isn't like flipping a switch, though. Consumers have finely tuned BS meters, which means companies that pretend to care without practicing what they preach will be punished in the town square of social media. With this in mind, what's the secret to authentic CSR that engages Millennials?

Show the World You Care

Many brands take a simple (and wrong) approach to advertising their CSR. They passively advertise the fact that they care, plastering their websites, packaging, and advertising with verbiage like "5 percent of proceeds go toward cancer research."

Those brands essentially tell consumers, "By purchasing this, you are participating in our cause. Good for you!" Similar to billboards on the highway, though, this passive approach rarely leads to increased engagement. Even die-hard devotees of fair-trade practices might not look closely enough at a brand's packaging to discover that the brand aligns with a cause they care about. When even the most ardent supporters of a shared mission don't notice your brand, something is deeply wrong.

I commend any brand that donates a portion of its proceeds to charitable causes or only uses ethically sourced materials. Those things are hard to do in a cutthroat market. But if all those brands do is talk about their CSR initiatives, they miss many better opportunities to drive awareness about themselves and their causes.

There are endless ways to show — not tell — the world about your brand's commitment to a higher purpose. At the very least, a brand with fair-trade CSR initiatives could send a camera crew down to Guatemala to interview its partner farmers and then create some engaging content around the initiative. Even better, that company could incorporate interactive elements into its CSR program. That might sound great, but it's not enough.

For shining examples of successful CSR (and CSR-based marketing), look no further than Patagonia. As an outdoor apparel and equipment brand, Patagonia expresses its love for the environment in several creative and engaging ways — starting with its website.

Upon the first visit to the company's homepage, it's apparent that the brand is serious about its CSR. You don't even have to scroll down to realize that Patagonia wants to help its customers save the world or that it hopes the products it sells will help make that goal a reality (rather than the other way around).

Over the years, the company has generated countless articles and videos about its social and environmental passions. Posts about nature, fair trade, and environmental events litter the company's blog. Patagonia doesn't just generate one-way content, though: It goes out of its way to create a two-way street of interactions between the brand and customers. Patagonia empowers its fans to live by their own values and principles, enabling both sides to work together to tackle the issues they care about.

Patagonia created a program called Action Works[81], for example, which serves as a matchmaker for cause-minded consumers. Visitors enter their location details on the Action Works site, specifying the genres of causes that matter to them. In exchange, they receive a list of organized opportunities they can join.

Patagonia's approach to CSR is not salesy nor advertorial in any sense. There are no allusions to purchasing outdoor wear or equipment in its CSR messaging — the brand openly states that advertising is "dead last" on its list of priorities.[82] Patagonia is more interested in solving problems in the world and providing experiences for like-minded customers.

Some might call this aversion to advertising an anti-growth strategy[83], but I call it genius. This proactive-yet-grassroots approach to CSR has made Patagonia founder Yvon Chouinard a billionaire[84] while enabling the brand to create an army of brand fanatics. Patagonia doesn't spend millions of dollars on traditional ads because it doesn't have to. The company's cause-driven brand identity fuels deep, emotional connections with consumers — and those connections repeatedly lead consumers back to the brand.

The type of brand fanaticism Patagonia has inspired is the holy grail of marketing. Companies that achieve this level of support don't need to woo audiences with expensive ads, celebrity spokespeople, or margin-eating coupons. These are the folks who buy from you regardless of how the economy is doing. They are part of your tribe. In the current era of prioritized peer recommendations, you need as many brand fanatics in your corner as you can create to help drive word-of-mouth marketing in social networks (both online and offline).

Fanaticism requires some level of devotion, which doesn't develop overnight. Patagonia has spent the past 40-plus years transforming itself into a CSR powerhouse. You won't reach the same level of success in a few months, but you can take steps today to start that process for your brand.

My agency has spent several years working with KaBOOM!, a Washington, D.C.-based nonprofit that provides recreational areas and equipment for children in underserved neighborhoods. These kids often don't have safe places to play, and their playground equipment tends to be either outdated, broken, or nonexistent. KaBOOM! comes in, builds a great playground in a single workday, and leaves behind a better neighborhood.

The company's system is unique: It leverages funding and volunteer labor provided by corporate sponsors and local partners to transform empty lots into play spaces in less than 24 hours. When companies partner with KaBOOM!, they create stronger local connections and show their communities that they care.

We partnered with Target and KaBOOM! as part of their KaBOOM!

Play Everywhere Tour. That partnership affected more than 10,000 people across four cities.

Because CSR initiatives like these can also inspire employees to be socially responsible[85], Target did more than just fund the partnership. It also sent out brand representatives to build these immersive experiences and interact with kids and parents. I have no doubt that those parents noticed and appreciated the major role Target played in providing fun, new spaces for their kids to play.

For a brand that positions itself as an affordable, one-stop shopping destination, this partnership makes perfect sense for Target. It's a great way to show the brand's audience that it truly cares about the health and well-being of its communities.

> *KaBOOM!, since its inception, has been about building infrastructure and building playgrounds. Years ago, we decided to broaden that category and include other activities like the huge grassroots event we call Play Everywhere, which is all about playing anywhere.*
>
> *Play Everywhere is committed to helping make play the easy choice for families. We have people exercising, we have dancing, playing games, and we are promoting fun. Families hanging out, being active, and playing together is what it's all about.*
>
> *—KaBOOM!*

Imagine if Target had simply written a check to KaBOOM! and advertised the partnership on its website. A few people might have noticed, and even fewer might have clicked a link to read more about it. The amount of awareness and emotional engagement that Target received from touring the country with KaBOOM!, however, far exceeds anything it might have gained from a passive sponsorship.

This mobile tour and CSR mission worked so well for Target because of the natural connection between the company's identity and its social mission. Just like Tide helps people wash their clothes and Duracell provides batteries during a power outage, Target invests in the community that supports its stores by buying products.

To create fanatics and show those business-killing Millennials that you're one of the good guys, you must do what these savvy brands did: Find a relevant niche and be authentic in your pursuit of CSR initiatives.

Find a Cause That Sticks

Fortunately, an authentic cause is always within reach. The world today offers brands thousands upon thousands of worthy causes to support, though this abundance of options does not mean that any old cause will do. Picking the "best" cause from a list often leads to picking the most PR-friendly one, which rarely resonates with the brand's purpose and usually triggers the audience's BS meter.

CSR should not be a PR ploy to drive profits and sell products. It should be a natural, honest extension of a business. In other words, your chosen cause must fit into your company's mission and vision.

To create a list of relevant, viable CSR options, start with the obvious question: "Which causes are important to our organization?" Note that this question is not the same as "Which causes matter to our consumers?" That comes later.

The most important component of an authentic outreach effort is internal buy-in. If the people funding and executing the program are not passionate about the problem the brand hopes to solve, the CSR initiative is doomed before it begins. Brand representatives at outreach events must possess genuine enthusiasm for what they do, or they will almost certainly trigger consumers' BS alarms. Even if fellow champions of the cause appreciate your involvement and contributions, they won't reward you with fanaticism just for showing up. They expect honest and heartfelt dedication — the kind of commitment that only arises from authentic CSR.

To discover what your company cares about, talk with the people who work there. Poll team members and assemble a list of every cause they say is important to them. Group that large list of causes into broad categories, such as environmental, local, and social justice. Only after compiling this broad list can you ask the big question: "Which of these causes will resonate best with our consumers?"

Don't ask your employees to guess what consumers want, though. Ask customers directly. Turn the ideation process for your next CSR initiative into an interactive experience. Put a poll on your website and social channels, ask your email list, and invite people to fill out in-person surveys— whatever it takes to gather as many consumer opinions as possible. You can then use those results to identify the cause that resonates both with your internal team and your target audience.

By following this selection method, you get the best of both worlds: Your brand tackles an initiative that matters to all involved parties, guaranteeing that both sides will be passionate about your CSR program. With that accomplished, you can hit the ground running and devote your brainpower to execution without worrying whether the concept will stick.

Occasionally, this polling exercise might not produce a cause that feels like a natural fit for your brand. You might need a little creative elbow grease to find the unique angle that sparks a connection, but you can make it work if your company and consumers want the same thing.

Here's how Duck Brand did just that.

As part of its CSR mission, Duck Brand decided to partner with a nonprofit called Project Love to tackle the problem of childhood bullying. On the surface, this cause appears to come out of left field. After all, what does duct tape have to do with bullying? Working with Duck Brand, we came up with a creative resolution to the apparent conflict. Given the adhesive nature of Duck Brand's main product, we decided to call the campaign "Stick Together."[86] We worked to show kids that they could join forces to combat bullying at their schools — helping them see that sticking together made them stronger.

Like the professional field trips I mentioned earlier in the book, we created a mobile experience inside an RV that visited elementary and middle schools across America. We provided a convenient, impactful event for students at each stop, seizing the opportunity to talk with kids about bullying and how they can prevent it. We used Duck Brand duct tape to illustrate how when people (or strips of tape) stick together, it's nearly impossible for anything — even the meanest bully in the world — to pull them apart.

After the Duck Tape bus tour was on the road for a couple years — going from retail outlet to retail outlet singing the gospel of Duck Tape — we stepped back and said: "Okay, we've hit all of our desired retailers. What are we going to do with this asset that we are not ready to retire?"

We wanted to build a program we believed in that our product could naturally help to support. At schools, we taught children that sticking together could help against bullies. The experiential part that resonated is that we used our product to show how the kids could stick together by sticking tape together and showing how hard it is to tear apart. The feedback we received from the children, teachers, and administrators was so positive.

—Duck Tape

These school visits ended up being incredibly experiential activities. The more pieces of tape we stick together, the harder they were to pull apart. Watching kids yank on the tape with all their might is beyond adorable, and seeing them have an "A-ha" moment when they make the connection between tape and friendship is uniquely rewarding.

At the end of the discussion and demonstration, we asked kids to make a pledge to "stick together" against bullying. They did so by writing their names on pieces of Duck Tape and then stuck the tape on a massive anti-bullying banner that hangs in their schools.

Kids enjoyed the experience because it took them out of their day-to-day classroom routine and provided something different. Much like B2B decision makers, students learned something important in an environment where they never felt like we were teaching them a lesson. Even though Duck Brand's anti-bullying CSR mission and our mobile tour never tried to sell any tape, the adults involved in the experience (parents and teachers) left with positive feelings and an emotional connection with Duck Brand.

Duck Brand and the prevention of bullying didn't have much in common when this initiative started. The people who worked at Duck Brand wanted to make a difference in the lives of children, and Project

Love was eager to help them achieve that dream. By the time we finished our "Stick Together" tour, Duck Brand became synonymous with kids standing up against bullies.

With a little creativity, your brand can do the same. Companies can connect to most causes — that's the easy part. The real challenge is identifying a cause that both your team and your target audience feel is worthy of their dedication. Once you discover that common ground, you can begin the creative process and create an impactful, authentic CSR initiative.

For the Long Haul

Cause marketing and corporate social responsibility are not fads — these concepts have existed for ages. Thanks to the rise of digital technology and the Millennial generation, the spotlight is shining brighter than ever before in this arena.

That bright spotlight reveals flaws as quickly as it reveals successes, though. When a brand halfheartedly commits to a cause or begins a CSR initiative with money in mind, consumers notice. For modern audiences, the only thing worse than a company that doesn't care about the world is a company that *pretends* to care.

Effective cause marketing sparks emotional connections like nothing else, and it rarely feels like marketing. Don't miss an opportunity to share a meaningful mission with your customers. Follow the polling process outlined earlier in this chapter to identify an authentic area where your brand can help, and then find proactive ways to make a difference in people's lives. Involve your audience to create an emotional connection, but leave the sales language at home — focus solely on what you and your customers can do to make the world a better place. Before long, your customers will see your brand as a reflection of the better parts of themselves.

You don't have to promote features and benefits. You don't need coupons, swag, samples, or anything else. You don't have to say, "Our brand is the best because we care!" Show people through your actions that you are passionate about the same causes they value — and that you're ready to do something about it.

CHAPTER 9

Spark Activism

"Stritzke's theory is that Americans are seeking "something more" than a simple deal when they shop. Instead, customers are seeking connection. If they identify with a company's values, customers reward that company with their loyalty." —Kate Taylor, correspondent, Business Insider

Up to this point, the experiential examples I've mentioned have successfully aligned brands with causes in engaging ways. Each example covered how a brand rolled up its sleeves to play an active role in a community or place of need. Tide and Target didn't just talk the talk — they walked the walk. Both brands cast aside marketing in favor of authentic devotion to a cause. In Patagonia's case, the brand provided resources that empowered customers to follow suit if they chose to do so.

These companies show the world that they care through experiential corporate social responsibility initiatives with authentic ties to the brand. In doing so, they hope consumers will follow their lead and form emotional connections along the way. They deserve praise for their genuine efforts to make the world a better place, but there is another element of

CSR outreach we haven't covered: consumer activism.

Say you're on your monthly dog food run to PetSmart. You have 25 pounds of kibble in your cart along with an assortment of treats, bones, and toys that your dog most certainly will destroy before he eats his next bowl of food. Maybe you have a cat, too, so you pick up a scratching post in a last-ditch effort to save your couch from Fluffy's claws.

You push your cart to the check-out lane and await your turn. As you engage in a staring contest with a teacup Chihuahua in another customer's purse, you overhear the cashier ask the front customer a question: "Would you like to help end pet homelessness by donating a dollar to PetSmart charities?"

That customer — who, judging by the large scratching post in his cart, shares your couch woes — naturally says yes. Why wouldn't he? It's only a dollar, and he doesn't want any animals to go hungry. Plus, the cashier asked *so* nicely. The lady with the Chihuahua goes next. Even though her dog continues to give you the stare of death, she happily agrees to donate another $1. People in the line next to you do the same thing. By the time you reach the register, you personally have witnessed at least $5 worth of donations to end pet homelessness.

Maybe you're the type of person who politely declines whenever someone asks you for a spur-of-the-moment donation. Regardless of your personal preferences, you just watched five other people agree to donate — and there are plenty of people waiting in line behind you. On top of that, this is a cause you care about: You adopted your dog from a shelter, and you love him enough to spend $15 to buy an oversized tennis ball. When you finally get to the front of the line, do you risk looking like a jerk by declining a meager $1 donation? Of course not.

Not only did you defend your status as a pet lover in front of your fellow shoppers, but you also did something you feel good about. You took a stand, making a tangible contribution to ending pet homelessness — even though you normally don't do that sort of thing.

Why does PetSmart's campaign work so well? This brand takes its CSR efforts a step beyond most of the examples we've discussed so far. The cashiers here don't just promote a social mission; they empower shoppers to adopt the cause as their own. This creates an experience and an emotional connection that puts consumer activism at the center, providing an excellent foundation for our next topic: how to get consumers to own your CSR initiative.

All You Have to Do Is Ask

Let's take a closer look at why PetSmart gets so many "yes" responses to its donation requests.

This campaign's consistent success aligns with many of the concepts we've already discussed. PetSmart's target audience is obviously in the right state of mind. They are surrounded by pet-related products, adoptable animals, and fellow pet lovers. They also just spent a solid 30 minutes filling a cart with pet food and toys.

Further, the timing of the request is impeccable. These people couldn't be more primed for pet-driven happiness. Thanks to the cashier, this is a human-to-human question that adds an extra layer of emotional involvement and accountability. You can't just ignore this request — if you want to decline the request, you have to look the cashier in the eyes and say, "No, I don't want to donate to help homeless kittens."

Psychology explains why we feel more compelled to agree when we speak face to face. According to a study published in 2017[87], participants were more likely to complete a survey when asked in person rather than via email. In fact, the study discovered that asking six people in person was just as effective as emailing a group of 200 individuals.

Imagine what would happen if PetSmart took a passive route like so many other retailers. You stand in line and never hear the cashier ask anyone to donate. When you get to the front and swipe your card, the machine — not the cashier — asks whether you want to donate. The touchscreen offers a green "yes" button and a red "no" button.

This approach would be passive and emotionless. There's no social pressure because nobody in line knows what anyone else clicks. As someone who normally declines this kind of solicitation, you reflexively hit "no" as soon as you realize it's a request for a donation. You probably don't even notice the recipient of the donation. You leave with a dollar saved, and PetSmart runs a less effective CSR initiative.

At this point, you're probably thinking about how easy brick-and-mortar retailers have it. They might be able to ask their customers to participate in a cause with ease, but what about the rest of us? What can e-commerce brands and B2B companies, which do not target a captive audience, do to involve their customers in CSR?

Fear not. As long as your brand authentically aligns itself with a cause and shows the world it is truly dedicated to solving that problem, you are pushing the right emotional buttons to spur activism and form connections. All you need to do is ask the right question in the right way.

Consider another established outdoor brand, REI, as a prime example. Since 2015, the company has activated a fantastic CSR campaign called "Opt Outside" that it hosts every Black Friday. On the biggest shopping day of the year, REI asks consumers a simple question: "Will you go out with us?"

No, that's not a request for a date. Rather than profit handsomely from the madness of Black Friday — which the company could easily do — REI chooses not to put anything on sale. In fact, REI chooses not to do anything at all. The retailer shuts down its corporate headquarters, distribution centers, and physical stores. REI pays its 12,000-plus employees to take a day off to enjoy the great outdoors, and it invites the rest of the world to join the fun. According to the company, more than 1.4 million people and 170 other organizations joined REI in shunning the holy day of capitalism in 2016.[88]

A store telling consumers not to go shopping on the biggest shopping day of the year seems insane, right? It's actually not that crazy. Black Friday might mean big money for retailers, but it's still just one day. More importantly for REI, it's a day that stands in direct opposition to the company's core values.

Black Friday is all about consumerism, gadgets, and creature comforts. It's a far cry from the freedom, simplicity, and love of Mother Nature that REI promotes. Those values draw people to the brand, which means REI shines in its mission by taking an anti-consumerism stance via Opt Outside. Not only does the brand stay true to its outdoorsy identity, but this annual event authentically embodies a CSR ideal REI shares with its target audience. Because REI prioritizes its core values more than short-term profits, it effectively tugs at its audience's heartstrings and forms an emotional connection that creates brand fanatics.

Beyond that (and more to the point at hand), REI's campaign drives activism. The moral of Opt Outside is not "We hope you care more about the environment now than you used to." Nor is it "We hope you now recognize the perils of consumerism." Rather, Opt Outside is a cut-and-dry physical movement. If you went to a mall on Black Friday, you didn't participate; if you went to a park and enjoyed the great outdoors, you did.

The people who participate in Opt Outside don't pay REI anything, and the company certainly loses money by giving every employee the day off. Despite those minor losses, it gains something far more important: the respect of its fans, who join the brand in its movement and reaffirm that they share REI's values.

Make a Trade

If you're a parent, you know there is a fine line between a bribe and a trade.

In a bribe, a father promises to give his son a pack of Skittles if the son agrees to mow the lawn. In a trade, that same father promises to teach his son how to drive a manual transmission if the son will teach him how to fix a laptop.

On the surface, these exchanges appear to be similar propositions. Each party gets something in exchange for something else. Bribes and trades are fundamentally different, though, and companies must understand that distinction if they want to spark activism and develop brand fanatics.

Let's return to the example of the son and the father. In the bribe scenario, the son gets a bag of Skittles, and the dad gets a (hopefully) pristine lawn. Depending on the size of the yard, the dad might need to spend $40 or more to get a professional to do the same job. Skittles cost significantly less than $40, so they represent a far better deal for the father. Candy isn't the best reward, though. Sugar carries numerous negative health effects, and any dad who is trying to instill healthy habits in his son might feel guilty about trading $40 of manual labor for a fleeting sugar rush.

Bribes like this one often create an imbalance of value. Not only that, but the currency used to spur the desired action (the Skittles) also leaves one party feeling happier than the other.

Let's move on to the trade between our hypothetical father and son. In my earlier example, the father teaches the son how to drive a car with a manual transmission. The son can show off in front of his Gen Z friends — who potentially have never seen a stick shift — and take his dad's 1972 Chevelle the next time he goes on a date. *Maybe.* The father, meanwhile, can save time, money, and trouble once his son teaches him how to uninstall the 17 toolbars the computer added seemingly on its own.

Unlike an unbalanced bribe, the trade is a fair exchange. Both parties emerge with something useful, and everyone wins.

How does this relate to marketing? Brands try to bribe consumers all the time with rebates, discounts, and freebies: "Order now and get a second ShamWow for free! Just pay processing and handling." These tactics can work, but more often flop. If someone doesn't want to buy one ShamWow, the offer of a second one won't magically help this person overcome that hesitation — much less become a loyal customer.

Branded bribery is a desperate move aimed at low-hanging fruit: customers who only want cheap or free stuff. These folks are the opposite of brand fanatics. They wait until clearance sales to pull out their wallets, they won't wait in line at your next product launch, and they won't put a sticker with your logo on their laptop. Sticking to the bargain bin works fine for people who pinch pennies for retirement, but consumer brands that target this group will fail to turn a profit or form emotional connections.

Trades, on the other hand, allow brands to identify their fanatics and inspire them to become activists. Let's look at the time my company worked with Disney to create a highly successful trade proposition.

In 2010, we helped Disney activate an experiential CSR program called "Give a Day, Get a Disney Day." In return for completing a day of service at one of several participating charities, Disney agreed to give volunteers a free one-day ticket to a Disney park. Pretty good deal, right? Volunteers who didn't use their tickets could even donate them to other charities. Disney hoped to inspire 1 million people to volunteer by the end of the first year of the campaign; we achieved that goal in 67 days.

What was the secret? We started by hitting consumers from all angles to maximize awareness about the promotion. The program was fully integrated with PR, online and offline advertising, a partnership with ABC's "Extreme Home Makeover," and even a viral video starring the Muppets. We also worked with several Disney brand ambassadors to boost awareness of the promotion and get people excited about a possible trip to Disney. The campaign was a huge success, earning numerous accolades during the 2010 PRO Awards.[89]

Our activation helped, but the marketing tactics weren't the core reason behind the campaign's success. This promotion spread like wildfire because it wasn't a bribe. If consumers wanted a free day at the park, they had to spend eight hours giving back to a reputable cause.

Disney set a high bar — this wasn't some cheap giveaway. Only people who truly cared about their causes would sign up to volunteer; fortunately for Disney, more than a million did. Consumers already had an affinity for Disney and their chosen nonprofits, so combining the two passions created its own kind of magic.

Let's break down the value of the trade. First, tickets to Disney parks are far from cheap. Costs vary depending on the location, but let's assume a conservative average of $75 for the purposes of this assessment. It doesn't take a math prodigy to figure out that Disney gave up more than $75 million of free tickets in only 67 days.

That's a lot of potential revenue that never hit Disney's pocket. Like our friends at Anheuser-Busch and NASCAR I mentioned earlier in the book, Disney would need a complex formula to prove the value of this campaign to the C-suite. Right?

Not really. While the primary goal of the program was to promote and provoke volunteerism in America, the secondary goal was to drive traffic to Disney parks. With that in mind, consider this: How many people spend only one day at Disney? And how many people go to Disney alone?

Unless the volunteer lived next door to a park, you can safely assume the recipient of a one-day pass intended to purchase additional tickets to make the most of his or her trip. While some individuals probably take solo trips to Disney, most people prefer to travel with friends and loved ones. Not only did volunteers need to purchase additional tickets for themselves, but they also needed to buy more tickets for their groups — even if their fellow travelers earned their own one-day passes. Once inside the parks, those 1 million visitors still purchased plenty of food, souvenirs, and other Disney offerings. This campaign was far from a loss leader for Disney; it was a brand builder that fortified emotional connections with audience members.

Trades like the one Disney offered to volunteers are a great way to spur activism. The people who received tickets didn't feel like they had been tricked into spending more money — nor did they feel like the offer was impersonal. They earned their tickets by contributing to causes that mattered to them. This wasn't a sign-up bonus that anyone could grab on a whim. It took dedication and planning to earn a ticket, and the million-plus people who went to a Disney park because of the promotion never felt like they got the raw end of the deal.

Even if your brand offers a free product in exchange for activism, you can make up the difference with a little creativity. Disney had it easy — park visitors naturally spend more money to attend — but other brands can turn an earned giveaway into a profitable exchange. You could offer discounts on accessories, limited-time lower rates, or another bonus relevant to the products or services you provide.

The important thing is ensuring the exchange is fair for both parties. If you ask for activism, be prepared to give up something of value in exchange. Not all trades should be designed with side profits in mind. Your goal is to make people feel like they partnered with your brand to make a difference in the world. In the long term, that emotional connection between their passion and your CSR initiative is more valuable than any coincidental sales.

Empower the Instinct to Act

Modern consumers want to be activists. They want to see themselves as forces of good in the world, and your brand can provide the spark they need to take the next step. Empower your target audience members to act on their altruistic urges by providing them with the two key components we covered in this chapter.

First, speak to them through human interactions. Don't limit your call to action to the digital realm and expect an overwhelming response. People respond more positively to propositions made through human-to-human connections. Much like a cashier at PetSmart, all you have to do is ask.

Second, propose a fair trade. Bribes only encourage people to do the bare minimum to secure the promised reward. When the exchange is over, the other party forgets it ever happened. Trades create value for both sides, especially when both the work and the reward resonate with the audience's beliefs. When you engage in a trade, you plant the seeds of a connection that grows beyond the initial exchange into a longer and more fruitful partnership.

By combining a human touch and an equal trade, you can transform would-be activists into empowered champions of your CSR efforts. It's important to note that your brand might not see the financial benefits of this connection immediately. But as you grow your audience of fanatics and start to see the goals of your CSR become reality, you will realize the true potential of these emotional connections.

Predicting the Future of Experiential Marketing

In the next 20 years, our experiential industry could very well take over all of marketing. At that point, everything will be digital and human interaction will be a rarity. To meet the needs of that digital future, though, experiential marketing *must* keep growing and evolving.

Today, we work with a handful of brands that I never knew existed until they called us. They weren't even on our radar. I find it incredible that they were willing to pick up the phone and say, "Hey! We want to talk about working with you guys!"

It definitely shows how versatile experiential marketing can be for any business in any industry. This is happening more and more in the B2B space, where experiential marketing has tremendous potential for growth — and where storytelling and "A-ha" moments are sometimes absent.

When you think about the future of experiential marketing, consider this: Sellers of every product from the dawn of time have depended on human interactions to close deals. What we're doing isn't new. If anything, it's the foundation of the entirety of marketing and communication. Other media, such as digital channels, deliver only a portion of a message. Conversely, experiential delivers the whole story *every* time. Some might call it an old-school approach, but I call it smart and effective.

The Oscar Mayer Wienermobile and the Budweiser Clydesdales are experiential activations that have persisted for more than 80 years. In some ways, you could consider them the first mobile marketing tours. Their novelty is not what defines them, though — it's their *method*. Those brands are willing to take that extra step to meet customers where they are, allowing these experiences to create authentic emotional connections that have continued to deliver year after year.

As we move into the future, technology will become increasingly important to the success of experiential marketing. We're just beginning to dabble in VR, and we're certain to encounter new and more engaging social media platforms. Although digital channels might seem disconnected from real-life experiences, online components have allowed the experiential industry to expand its reach far beyond past limitations. Moving forward, I am confident that our industry will continue to partner with social media to great effect, and brand marketers will keep looking for ways to prove ROI in that virtual space.

My greatest wish for our industry — and our company specifically — is for more B2B businesses to turn to experiential marketing. Today's experiential marketing results revolve around building a brand, which can get lost in the murky waters of shares, likes, and engagement. With B2B, however, the benefits are clearer. Before this wish can come true, though, B2B leaders must loosen their grips on the old status quo of trade shows and take their brave first steps into experiential. It isn't as daunting as it seems, but even a small step can feel insurmountable for companies set in their ways.

But on to the big question: What comes next? In all honesty, if you are challenged with increasing sales or driving more effective engagement for your brand (or your client's brand), I would love for you to finish this book, pick up the phone, and call me. I am eager to walk you through your first experiential campaign or help you refresh one you've tried in the past. That's a tall order, though, so I'll settle for something more realistic.

Use what you have learned in this book to strike up conversations about experiential marketing. I have a genuine passion for this industry, but I want to know what *you* think. Where do you struggle to connect with your consumers? What challenges does your brand have? How can experiential marketing solve those challenges for you?

Let's continue the conversation together, the way humans have talked to one another for thousands of years. Whether we experience those conversations face-to-face or on a platform yet to be revealed, I look forward to a lively (and productive) discussion.

Steve Randazzo, President
Pro Motion, Inc.
www.promotion1.com
636-449-3163
steve.randazzo@promotion1.com
linkedin.com/in/steverandazzo/

About the Author

Steve Randazzo is the founder and president of Pro Motion, Inc., a trusted, award winning experiential marketing agency located in St. Louis, Missouri since 1995. Pro Motion helps B2B and B2C brands and Agency partners cut through the clutter and drive real tangible results. With over 30 years of experience in the industry, Steve has lead his agency's relationships with big-name clients, including, The Walt Disney Company, Dr Pepper-Snapple Group, Hewlett-Packard, Duck Tape, Anheuser-Busch, Fiskars, Citgo, NBA, Tractor Supply Company, and many top notch agency partners. Steve has over 50 published articles and is known as a thought leader in his industry. He has been awarded such accolades as Top 100 People You Should Know in St. Louis and one of Fortune Small Business' Best Bosses.

Pro Motion, Inc.
18405 Edison Ave.
Chesterfield, MO 63005

Twitter: @steverandazzo
Instagram: steve.randazzo
www.steve-randazzo.com

linkedin.com/company/pro-motion-inc
facebook.com/promotioninc/
Twitter: @ProMotionInc
Instagram: promotionexperiential

References

[1]EventTrack 2018, Seventh Annual Edition, "The Event & Experiential Marketing Industry Forecast & Best Practices Study," eventmarketer and Mosaic (https://drive.google.com/file/d/1IpcMTgdhZSCDQ8y06m-vgeX20y_eF-Vt/view)

[2]https://blog.bizzabo.com/event-marketing-2018-benchmarks-and-trends

[3]https://www.amazon.ca/Experience-Economy-Updated-Joseph-Pine/dp/1422161978

[4]http://www.annualreviews.org/doi/10.1146/annurev.ps.41.020190.002221

[5]https://hbr.org/2015/11/the-new-science-of-customer-emotions

[6]https://www.emarketer.com/Article/eMarketer-Lowers-US-TV-Ad-Spend-Estimate-Cord-Cutting-Accelerates/1016463

[7]https://www.ericsson.com/en/networked-society/trends-and-insights/consumerlab/consumer-insights/reports/tv-and-media-2016#keyfindings

[8]https://hbr.org/2014/03/how-to-deal-with-unfamiliar-situations

[9]https://www.brandwatch.com/2014/06/promotional-products-brand-recognition/

[10]http://corporate.qvc.com/documents/20536/164719/QVC+Fact+Sheet+Q4+3-9-17.pdf/ddc62f93-015e-48bd-be67-4c76e6d57db7

[11]https://www.emarketer.com/Article/What-Do-Teen-Influencers-Watch-on-YouTube/1015287

[12]https://retail.emarketer.com/article/us-shoppers-still-prefer-make-most-purchases-in-store/58dd8922ebd400061c80f3cf

[13]https://www.livescience.com/8426-brain-link-sounds-smells-memory-revealed.html

[14]http://www.autonews.com/article/20150511/RETAIL03/305119998/bmw-expands-event-marketing-after-success-in-14

[15]https://agencyea.com/thoughts/value-experiential-marketing/

[16]https://www.smartinsights.com/internet-advertising/internet-advertising-analytics/display-advertising-clickthrough-rates/

17https://research.hubspot.com/reports/why-people-block-ads-and-what-it-means-for-marketers-and-advertisers?hstc=93759874.032843caf5a36699bf437ae58b60b4f2.1510952734603.1510952734603.1510952734603.1&__hssc=93759874.1.1510952734603&__hsfp=3688941333

[18]https://www.huffingtonpost.com/entry/yes-there-are-too-many-ads-online-yes-you-can-stop_us_589b888de4b02bbb1816c297

[19]http://time.com/3858309/attention-spans-goldfish/

[20]http://www.nielsen.com/us/en/press-room/2015/recommendations-from-friends-remain-most-credible-form-of-advertising.html

[21]http://www.adweek.com/digital/why-influencer-marketing-is-the-new-content-king-infographic/

[22]https://www.sweetmarthas.com/about.html

[23]http://www.startribune.com/meet-sweet-martha-who-brings-in-4m-in-12-days-selling-cookies-at-the-fair/442433423/

[24]https://www.bloomberg.com/features/2016-sorority-fashion/

[25]https://www.oracle.com/corporate/pressrelease/oracle-retail-2025-032217.html

[26]https://papers.ssrn.com/sol3/papers.cfm?abstract_id=2832068

[27] http://www.ceir.org/2017-ceir-index-report-now-available

[28] http://www.houstonchronicle.com/business/article/OTC-attendance-down-as-offshore-loses-its-groove-11122942.php

[29] http://www.nationaljeweler.com/independents/trade-shows/5605-attendance-down-slightly-at-jck-las-vegas-2017

[30] http://www.chicagotribune.com/business/ct-chicago-loses-food-marketing-show-0929-biz-20160928-story.html

[31] https://www.techvalidate.com/product-research/frost-and-sullivan/facts/B31-028-1C6

[32] https://agencyea.com/news/agencyea-reveals-2019-state-of-experiential-marketing-with-new-research-findings/

[33] http://adage.com/article/media/nfl/305791/

[34] https://www.ncbi.nlm.nih.gov/pubmed/23881574

[35] http://www.partnershipactivation.com/sportsbiz/2009/4/17/mcdonalds-knocks-it-out-of-the-park-with-big-mac-land.html

[36] https://www.youtube.com/watch?v=rESCt1Te1VY

[37] https://www.youtube.com/watch?v=RaLecnMEX3E

[38] https://agencyea.com/experiential-marketing-trends-in-2018/

[39] https://www.thestreet.com/story/14283620/1/corporate-america-wants-a-piece-of-the-mayweather-mcgregor-action.html

[40] http://www.espn.com/boxing/story/_/id/20535309/estimated-50-million-people-watched-floyd-mayweather-jr-vs-conor-mcgregor-fight

[41] https://www.marketo.com/analyst-and-other-reports/the-state-of-engagement/

[42]https://www.freeman.com/resources/brand-experience-a-new-era-in-marketing

[43]http://www.bbc.com/news/business-22066153

[44]http://brandsandfilms.com/2012/11/product-placement-in-pictures-skyfall/

[45]https://www.youtube.com/watch?v=vuMvhJaWIUg

[46]https://www.youtube.com/watch?v=N29tEszlgQU

[47]http://markdebrand.com/experiential-marketing-statistics/

[48]https://www.usnews.com/news/blogs/data-mine/2014/06/28/which-shirts-and-shoes-are-winning-the-world-cup

[49]https://www.soccer.com/guide/adidas-fifa-world-cup-ball-history

[50]https://www.usatoday.com/story/sports/soccer/2014/06/08/adidas-and-nike-jostle-for-edge-at-the-world-cup/10198823/

[51]http://www.adweek.com/brand-marketing/ad-day-nike-launches-risk-everything-campaign-ahead-2014-world-cup-156680/

[52]https://www.forbes.com/sites/markfidelman/2014/07/01/nike-is-dominating-the-world-cup-heres-why/

[53]http://blg.mktg.com/2014/06/nike-risk-everything-winner-stays-2/

[54]https://www.theguardian.com/football/2018/jun/14/adidas-nike-world-cup-who-wins

[55]https://ftw.usatoday.com/2017/06/nike-cristiano-ronaldo-ad-adidas

[56]https://www.flickr.com/photos/promotioninc/5701619849/in/photostream/

[57]https://promotion1.com/project/cnn-election-express-yourself-tour/

[58]http://www.ducktapefestival.com/

[59] http://www.adweek.com/digital/bad-news-negative-headlines-get-much-more-attention/

[60] http://journals.sagepub.com/doi/full/10.1177/2054270414533323

[61] https://tide.com/en-us/about-tide/loads-of-hope/about-loads-of-hope

[62] https://www.ob.org/loads-of-hope-for-haiti/

[63] https://www.duracell.com/en-us/program/duracell-powerforward/

[64] http://www.smh.com.au/news/world/penns-rescue-attempt-springs-a-leak/2005/09/05/1125772436185.html

[65] https://www.huffingtonpost.com/sean-penn/mountain-of-snakes_b_146765.html

[66] http://abcnews.go.com/Entertainment/HurricaneKatrina/story?id=1702714&page=1

[67] https://www.cbssports.com/nfl/news/j-j-watts-final-fundraiser-total-for-hurricane-harvey-relief-tops-37-million/

[68] https://www.cbssports.com/nfl/news/j-j-watt-named-walter-payton-man-of-the-year-for-hurricane-harvey-relief-efforts/

[69] https://www.mlb.com/news/yadier-molina-returns-to-puerto-rico-for-aid/c-264941760

[70] https://www.usatoday.com/videos/money/2017/02/24/millennials-killing-department-stores/98187754/

[71] https://nypost.com/2016/04/15/millennials-are-killing-the-movie-business/

[72] https://www.bloomberg.com/news/articles/2017-04-04/young-americans-are-killing-marriage

[73] https://www.entrepreneur.com/slideshow/306560

[74] https://www.goldmansachs.com/insights/pages/millennials-changing-consumer-behavior.html

[75] https://www.thecut.com/2017/03/why-millennial-pink-refuses-to-go-away.html

[76] http://www.conecomm.com/news-blog/new-cone-communications-research-confirms-millennials-as-americas-most-ardent-csr-supporters

[77] http://www.pewresearch.org/fact-tank/2015/05/11/millennials-surpass-gen-xers-as-the-largest-generation-in-u-s-labor-force/

[78] http://www.conecomm.com/research-blog/2016-millennial-employee-engagement-study

[79] http://bas.sagepub.com/content/38/3/268.abstract

[80] https://www.epa.gov/superfund

[81] https://www.patagonia.com/actionworks/about/

[82] http://adage.com/article/cmo-strategy/advertising-dead-priority-patagonia/245712/

[83] https://www.newyorker.com/business/currency/patagonias-anti-growth-strategy

[84] https://www.forbes.com/sites/danielasirtori/2017/03/20/from-climber-to-billionaire-how-yvon-chouinard-built-patagonia-into-a-powerhouse-his-own-way/#185284c9275c

[85] https://www.forbes.com/sites/forbescommunicationscouncil/2018/07/13/companies-can-improve-the-world-how-csr-and-marketing-tie-the-knot/#1f4cf3523082

[86] https://www.duckbrand.com/promotions/sticktogether

[87] https://www.sciencedirect.com/science/article/pii/S002210311630292X

[88]https://www.rei.com/blog/news/optoutside-will-you-go-out-with-us

[89]http://www.donnaspromotalk.com/promos_2010_pro_awards_top_honors_go_to_disneys_give_a_day_get_a_disney_day/

CPSIA information can be obtained
at www.ICGtesting.com
Printed in the USA
LVHW090847170320
650282LV00001B/5/J

9 781733 874502